For
Steffen
Nicholas
Daniel

Contents

Going Back to Say Goodbye (1986)

Hilary didn't beat about the bush, the night she phoned. "It's spread into his brain," she said. "It's more or less everywhere. We think you should come quickly."

I wasn't shocked but suddenly scared. I arranged flights.

I didn't know the new house. It was smaller, sunnier than the home we'd moved to in 1964, when Dad was transferred to head office in Johannesburg, but full of the same stuff I knew from my boyhood. And William was still standing in the kitchen, greyer, shorter but familiar. I shook his soft hand.

The day after I arrived, my mother led my sisters and me into the Hillbrow Hospital. "We're going to bring him home, no matter what they say. They should never have done that stupid surgery. I'll sign whatever they want!"

He sat on the edge of the bed while Mom fussed with his dressing gown and slippers and packed his few things. I eased him into a wheelchair and pushed him down the corridor and into a lift. At the front desk Mom told someone she was taking him home. They didn't seem at all concerned. We waited on the pavement while Hilary fetched her car.

I looked down at him. He was terribly pale and thin. He looked like someone who was going home to die.

I'd seen him just two years earlier. On his way back from metallurgical work in Venezuela, he'd visited us for a week at our place, north of Kingston. He and Carolyn watched the Olympics in Los Angeles on TV while I worked shifts at the hospital. He was warmer and more relaxed than I ever re-membered and he played sweetly with Stef, his five-year-old grandson and namesake. We had a good time together.

The airport shuttle bus left from the Days Inn and we got there a little early but he wanted to claim a window seat, so we hugged and kissed goodbye and he climbed aboard. I stood on the tar as he looked down at me. We'd both look away and then look back at each other. Every time we caught each other's gaze, he smiled. A smile of real affection.

I was deeply moved. I thought that, after all, he must have slowly grown fond of me. For years, we'd been estranged to some degree: politics, the army, dropping out, the push and shove of father and son. I'd left South Africa with bitterness towards him. I thought he'd be smugly content, when, after a few months, I came home with my tail between my legs. But I didn't. I stayed overseas. First in Holland, and then in Canada.

Hilary drove up to the hospital entrance and we got him comfortably settled in the back of the car. I sat beside him. After a few blocks he said that we were going too fast, it was too bumpy. When I looked at him he gave me a small, self-deprecating smile.

Within a week his thin white stubble and shrunken cheeks had begun to unsettle Mom. He lay curled up on the bed in the spare room, silent except for a soft, whistling sound he made when he exhaled.

One morning she asked me to shave him; it would freshen him up, make him presentable. But when I suggested it might be tiring, she said sadly, "I know. Please, Kenneth. Do it for me. I don't like how he looks." She started crying. "He looks so terrible."

So we set up a basin and I put a new blade in his razor. "Dad," I said, "I want to clean you up, give you a shave." He nodded and allowed us to prop him up with cushions.

I had half his face done when he said, "Stop! I'm getting giddy! I want to lie back down."

I eased him down and then dabbed the soap off his whiskers. Outside, my mother whispered, "Well, at least we tried."

So for the last few days of his life he presented an odd spectacle to those who came to say goodbye. One side was the clean-shaven man we all recognised: father, husband, brother, friend. The other half was a white-bearded stranger. Someone who'd slid off a canvas by El Greco and into the bed against the wall. An old man with black, red-rimmed eyes who had appeared here, only to die.

He could have said something about what was happening, maybe that he was on his last legs, but he said nothing.

I touched him more in those weeks than I'd done in my entire life. And somehow that meant unequivocally it was over, that there was no hope. For as long as I'd known him, his body had been his alone, clothed, private and smelling of smoke. He was not a touching man and he didn't invite it. Now he barely noticed.

I rubbed his back, avoiding the jagged shark-bite of the lung biopsy, and washed him gently between his legs. His penis lay folded and naked as a nestling. I was pretty sure I'd never seen it before. My gloved finger tingled as I inserted the Gravol suppositories.

Moments of lucidity became rare. He was visited by his two older half-brothers, gruff, rough men. They jostled awkwardly in the doorway, making placating noises. The eldest said hoarsely, "Hells bells! You're not looking too bad, my boy!"

My father, suddenly alert, muttered, "Who do you think you're kidding, Dick?"

And then those old men sat in the lounge in their flannels and ties and jackets and had tea. And they both had wet eyes when they kissed my mom goodbye. They called her "Jeannie".

Late one afternoon the neighbour's dog started barking at the back fence and my father yelled, with surprising vigour, "Someone, please, shoot that dog!"

We invited a family friend over, a furniture maker, and asked him to make a pine casket, simple and unvarnished. It's what Dad once said he wanted and Mom had remembered.

Then we all sat in the garden and felt the warmth of the sun on our backs. We spoke of hospice and autumn flowers and South African woods: tamboti, hardekool, stinkwood, kiaat.

In the afternoons our mother lay down on the carpet by his bed and slept.

My sisters waited. I waited as long as I could. I added a week to my stay, and then another. The doctor couldn't say and I decided to return to Canada.

On my last afternoon, as my sisters and mother sat in the

lounge, I went up the hallway to say goodbye. My suitcase was at the front door. I felt their sadness for me; they had a little more time, they could be surprised, but I had to say a formal farewell, there and then. I wouldn't see him again.

I should have said, "Dad, I'm not going to see you again. I want to say I love you before I go." Sat by his bed, held his hand, maybe stroked it. Or something like that. But I didn't. I stood there and said, "Well Dad, I've got to get back to the family. I'm afraid I've got to say 'cheerio'."

His eyes opened, unfocused and confused.

"Already! It seems you've only been here a day or two." Then he smiled. "How are you getting back, my boy? By boat?"

I said, "No, Dad. By plane." And I looked at him for one long instant and then kissed him on the top of his head as though he were a small, sleepy boy.

"Bye, Dad," I said. He smiled, and I turned away.

A Boyhood on the Mine
(1954–1961)

At the Beginning

After Gill was born we moved from Joburg to Stilfontein. I was four and Ingrid was two. Dad had worked at Rand Leases but now was going to a new mine called Hartebeesfontein. Everyone was excited, but I knew we were going a long, long way away. Both our grans and grandad came to say goodbye. Scruffy, our dog, didn't come with us because he wandered off one afternoon and never came home. I kept looking back as we drove off just in case he suddenly ran round a corner.

The moving van got lost and we stayed at someone's house for days until it came. De Mist Avenue was a brand-new road then and wasn't even tarred. The houses were new too. We moved into number 9 and Mom let me help her unpack the boxes. There were giant boulders and rocks in the front yard that gangs of natives first covered with piles and piles of ground and then planted with grass seed.

Dad was building a thing called a pilot plant and he had to work so hard that some nights he stayed at the mine. But always, just before he came home, Mom combed her hair and took off her apron.

She found the hall that the Methodists used for a church and Sunday school and started making friends and also finding new friends for us. She walked everywhere, pushing Gilly in the pram. We lived in the same house for the whole year before I started school. Then we moved just around the corner to 113 Van Riebeeck Drive. Even though we were close to the school I never, ever wanted to go. I begged to be allowed to stay home, but Dad said he'd go to jail if they didn't send me.

Mom took and fetched me the first week, but after that my friend Nev and I would walk to school after breakfast and hang around the door to our classroom. It was way safer there than in the playground. Gangs would chase you if you didn't watch it, and after the last bell sounded we'd run home, looking over our shoulders the whole way.

When I tell my mom what I remember from when I was little she says, "Aren't memories wonderful? They're so mysterious. They appear from simply nowhere!" She laughs and holds out her hands.

The Mining Game

The fathers of my friends go underground every day, but I don't say that my dad thinks it's boring work. He's a metallurgist, and he likes the reduction works and the mills and the chemicals so much that my mom sort of laughs and says he prefers the plant to our house. If someone asks him what he does, he says, "I'm in the mining game."

Stilfontein has three mines: Stilfontein, Buffelsfontein and Hartebeesfontein. Four, if you count Zandpan, but it belongs to Harties. They belong to different companies but we all live in the same town, plonked down between the Old Potch Road and the railway line that goes from Joburg to Kimberley. Headgears, rock piles and slimes dams are all around us, except for the veld on one side. It goes on forever, most probably all the way to Rhodesia.

The back of Dad's cigarette box always has rows of numbers written in pencil, and he uses an adding machine that also subtracts when you turn the handle backwards. The whole family has to keep quiet when he works at his desk on the weekend; otherwise he makes a mistake and starts yelling. He invents. Mr Smook, the mill foreman, showed me a small machine that measures something and said, "Your father thought that up and had it built by a tool-maker!" Now he's writing a paper about machines called "cyclones". They're called cyclones because they spin very fast and separate gold or uranium, I can't remember which.

He's always talking about pumps, tanks and flow charts. Everything is pumped: from one building to another, from tanks to cyclones, and, at the end, all the way to the slimes dam. If a pump breaks, he'll get a phone call, even in the middle of the night and he gets up and drives to the mine and then comes back furious at some "bloody idiot" or "shoddy workmanship".

"It'll set production back by days," he moans to my mom.

Once he got a call late at night and went to the plant and only came back at breakfast, stubbly and with red eyes. He whispered something to my mom, and after he went to sleep she told us that two men had been killed and others badly hurt when scaffolding on the side of a new building was blown down by a strong wind. She said that only a few days before she'd seen an owl flying in the garden and had a premonition something bad was going to happen, just like she did before Grandad died.

When there's an accident on the mine, either underground or on the surface, you hear the siren. You can hear it all over town and it goes on and on and everybody looks at everybody else. You get butterflies in your stomach. You even wonder if your friend's dad is dead. Grown-ups tell kids to pipe down or shut up and then whisper to each other. The phone keeps ringing. Someone always asks, "How many?", and after they get the answer they ask, "And Europeans?"

When you drive near the mine the first things you see are the concrete headgears and the black flywheels on top, turning one way to bring up rock or men and the other way to lower the empty skips or take the next shift below. Then you see the huge corrugated-iron buildings for the mills and tanks and crushers and the smelting works.

There are steep mountains of waste rock piled in the veld. Across the road the shunting yard is always full of freight cars painted like toys. *Cynamid* is written across lots of the tankers. Mostly what comes in is chemicals and dynamite.

You can walk around big, open tanks with slowly turning arms mixing up stuff. There are pipes and thick hoses running through pools of oily ground water. Natives in overalls and gumboots are everywhere. Usually a foreman is standing close by telling them what to do.

The scariest place, except for underground, is the sorter station. You climb up winding stairs for ages and come to a long narrow shed that slants down, high up above the crushers. If you look out, all you see is veld.

Everyone shouts because of the noise. A black rubber conveyor belt carries the rock along. Natives sitting on both sides pick out the pieces with no ore and throw them down the waste chutes. It's scary because the gangway is made of metal full of holes. You can look between your feet and see the ground way, way below. It's like walking on air and if you stop someone always says, "Don't look down!" My knees lock and I put my arms out to feel steady.

Cyanide is for gold and sulphuric acid is for uranium. There's a vinegary smell in all the buildings. I like standing in front of the big drums slowly turning towards me with spraying water and the uranium oxide peeling off and dropping in big slurpy bits into the trough. They call it yellowcake and it's not dangerous until it goes to America and becomes atom bombs.

Grown-ups say if you ask too many questions about uranium the police "pay you a visit" to find out if you're a Russian spy.

They smelt the gold in a special furnace. When it's molten the smelters first pour off the stuff called slag into a special flask and then the gold into moulds shaped like slanted bricks. The gold bubbles and splatters and spills, but the smelters wear fireproof suits and special helmets and use long tongs to hold the crucible. Afterwards they sweep up everything on the floor and save it to smelt the next time.

Every month the gold bars from the three mines are stacked in a special train that waits at Machavie Station or Koekemoer. Police with guns are locked inside a bulletproof carriage with the gold and they stay there all the way to the Rand Refinery.

Now and then on a weekend my dad takes us to the plant to show us "how it's coming along". Gillian and Hilary are too small to come, and stay with Linda, our babysitter. On our way there we drive past the open field where they have the mine dances. There's a wooden stand at one end where we sit and watch. Different tribes have different costumes and their own special dances. Pondos, Xhosas, Basutos, natives from Mozambique and Rhodesia. The Zulus are the scariest. They hammer the ground with their bare feet and move slowly towards us, swaying, singing and waving assegais.

Today we are going to see real Bushmen. Recruiters found them in Bechuanaland and brought them here because scientists say they can see green better than anyone else. They can spot small bits of gold ore in the rocks and save the mine tons of money.

I've read about them and my dad has told me lots. Long ago they painted pictures in caves all over South Africa, but we and the native tribes hunted them like animals and pushed them into the Kalahari Desert. They run all day following the spoor of a buck that's slowly dying from a poisoned arrow and they've got ostrich eggs filled with water buried all over the place. They remember exactly where they're hidden. Now they're slowly becoming extinct.

We climb up to the sorter station. There are rows of natives sitting at the conveyor belt and they stare at me and Ingrid, but Mom says they are not being rude. She says it's because they don't see their children for the whole year that they work on the mines. They have to leave their families behind when they come to work here.

I look for Bushmen but can't see any. You can't hear anything above the noise of the rocks and the crushers so I tug my dad's arm. He points to the end of the station. There's only one of them and I can hardly see him because his helmet is miles too big. He's tiny and his face is like a Chinaman's.

He sits there in his overalls with huge rubber pads on his hands and stares as the rocks go by. All the time we stand there, he doesn't look up once.

How We Got Here

Our family crest hangs right at the front door next to Grandad Smith's painting of two waterbuck. There are silvery wings on top of a helmet and underneath a shield that's got green water lilies and iron stakes painted on it. My dad got it from his dad who got it from his dad. All the way back to 1200-and-something.

A chieftain called Le Cocq swam across the moat and climbed the walls of Ruynsberg Castle in Holland to rescue Countess Ada. For his bravery, Count Dirk, Ada's brother, gave the chieftain his own coat of arms.

Le Cocq changed to de Kok long ago.

"Hey you, de Kok!" kids say. "You've got a big hairyback name. How come you're not at the rockspider school?" I'd explain, but they're stupid and walk away laughing like crazy.

I'd say, "My mother's maiden name is Smith. English, right?" Then I'd say the names of all the kids in our class with Afrikaans surnames: De Waal, Liebenberg, Abrahamse, Lourens. They all speak English at home, and that's why they're here at Strathvaal, at an English-medium school, and not at Stilfontein Laerskool.

In South Africa, first you're either black or white. And if you're white, you're either English or Afrikaans. There are others, like Greeks, Portuguese, Jews and Lebanese, but they count as English.

In 1854 my great-grandfather Pieter came to South Africa

from Holland and settled in the Orange Free State. His second-oldest son, my grandfather, was born in 1869 and died in Johannesburg in 1947, a year before my mom and dad were married. His name was Henri, the same as my second name.

He went bankrupt after the Boer War; first he lost the farm and then his hotel in Winburg. That part of the family wouldn't speak Afrikaans at all, but walked around Winburg in wooden clogs, talking Dutch: Hooghollands they called it. They blamed the Afrikaners for everything and moved to Johannesburg. From then on, the family only spoke English; Grandad stayed home and let my gran earn the money. He polished the children's shoes, dried peaches in the back yard and drank brandy.

Granny de Kok's maiden name is Van Niekerk, but her friends call her "Tolly" because her second name is Taillefere. Some of her ancestors were French Huguenots and she says that somewhere in France there's a buried treasure that belongs to us.

She was seventeen when she got stuck in the siege of Kimberley and had to eat horsemeat. After that she taught primary school in Winburg and married my grandfather when his first wife died of diphtheria. She must have been Afrikaans but now speaks English with a posh accent. She has a prickly white moustache and sits by the radio listening to love stories and the prices on the Johannesburg Stock Exchange.

Mom's side is the Smith side. Her grandfather Bill was a cockney who came out to South Africa in 1890. He was nineteen and worked as a propman in a theatre in Durban when he first arrived. That's where he met Maggie Stewart, our great-grandmother. Her family grew sugar cane but she was a "Gaiety Girl" in the same theatre. Someone who also liked her cut off Bill's thumb in a fencing match. But she still chose Bill and had twelve children in fifteen years.

In 1896 he took part in the Jameson Raid. My dad says Cecil Rhodes planned it all and that the whole gang were a bunch of bloody jingoes and were lucky they weren't hanged.

Mom says Great-grandad Bill was a small bully. That family loved singing and on Friday nights the sons would drink and box in the kitchen.

Grandad Smith loved my mom, the Queen and everything English. He drove a Morris and wouldn't buy anything made in Germany. He was a blacksmith first, but studied to be a health inspector. He really wanted to go to London once in his life, but didn't make it.

Gran Smith's maiden name is Rowles. Her father came from England with the troops to fight in the Boer War. He was in the veterinary corps and afterwards stayed on in South Africa and became a builder. His wife was a Dreyer, an Afrikaner. One of her relatives was the girlfriend of Robey Leibbrandt, the Nazi traitor. My dad says they should have hanged him from the tallest building in the Union.

When Great-grandad Rowles died in 1934, he had a military funeral and Mom says soldiers fired shots over his grave.

Granny Smith lives with us now at 156 Van Riebeeck. She came when Grandad died. She's got diabetes and angina but can't stop eating cakes and sweets. She loves chatting and playing cards – bridge, canasta, rummy, even Monopoly – so long as she's having fun. She hides chocolates in a biscuit barrel in her cupboard and an assortment box of sweets in her chest of drawers and bribes me to scratch her back.

Here in Stilfontein most of the managers and engineers are English, but my dad says that's slowly changing. The Afrikaners are starting their own mining companies and banks. They don't just want to be farmers or train conductors any more.

So of my eight great-grandparents, two are Dutch, three are English and three are Afrikaans. Everything's mixed up. That's how it works here. Some people end up speaking English and others Afrikaans.

Because of the Boer War and other stuff, English and Afrikaners don't like each other much. My dad's side of the family is not sure which side to be on. They think that lots of Afrikaners are "proper gawies" and only run the country because there are more of them. But they have a problem with English-speakers too, who think that England is their proper home and don't really understand or love South Africa.

Bike Licence

I thought it up. It was my plan. We'd go to the Licence Office the first day after New Year and be the first in line. I'd get the number one because it was my idea.

Dessington had sort of agreed to get the number two.

I borrowed my dad's travel alarm clock. When you snapped open the hard green case a gold clock was inside. At half past six in the morning, the second it rang I knew it was Friday 2 January 1960. The plan was under way. I pulled on my shorts and shirt, socks and shoes and tucked my pyjamas under the pillow. I tiptoed down the passage to the kitchen.

"Don't wake up the whole house! Especially Hilary. Please!" Mom had said the night before.

I poured a bowl of Post Toasties, added milk and lots of sugar and slurped it, looking out the window at a cloth bag of pegs swaying on the washing line. Behind that, the split-pole fence blocked out the Meyers' back yard. It was so early. The blue sky looked as though it went all the way to the South Pole.

The top of William's head moved across the bottom of the window. His key was in the back door. "Morning, William. Why're you up so early?" I asked.

He smiled and said, "Always, Massa. Happasix." For the first time I realised that he always got up this early and saw the day exactly like this, the house quiet, the yard empty and the lawn dark and cool.

I wondered what colour it would be this year, 1960. Last year's was green. A green square. My number seventy-eight was painted in black. A hopeless number. And under that one, the red diamond from 1958, number four hundred and seventeen. But in 1958, the first year I'd had a bike, I didn't know that the number was important, that the number meant something. Kids stood talking to each other on their bikes. "What's your number?" they'd ask and look down at your front wheel where the licence was attached. Your number means something serious to kids who ride all the time.

I opened the blue biscuit tin and stuck three of Mom's oatmeal cookies in my pocket. "You can take two," she'd said. I said goodbye to William, went through the back gate and quietly lifted one of the garage doors. I always watch the counterweights moving. Pipes filled with concrete on steel cables.

I wheeled my bike, a black Raleigh Sports three-speed with white mudguards, to the gate. It was nearly three years old but still my size. I made sure the gate was latched. Dad gets furious if one of us forgets. I gave the bike a push. Two quick steps alongside and then swing my leg over and go, go, go. I went flat out straight away. Speeding past all the houses, one after another, the curtains closed, everyone asleep. So quiet. Just the rushing of the tyres on the tar. Then suddenly a little black-and-white foxy snapping and bouncing behind his fence. Long curve and I lean down. Quick look right and left, through the stop street, back onto Van Riebeeck for one block and then turn into De Mist.

"Dessington!" He's standing by his bike, a Humber, looking

back with his mouth open like someone in a relay race. "Let's go!" No stopping, pedalling hard like there was a gang of rockies chasing us. Slowing a bit just before the park so we rode together past the Single Quarters and the hall where Ingrid and I used to go to Sunday school before they built the Methodist church.

Then down to the shopping centre, where all the shops were still shut: the Norvaal Bottle Store; Koekemoer Butchers; the chemist; the barber; Claude Mathieu, the jewellers; Stilfontein Supermarket, where Mom gets all of our stuff at the end of the month when my dad gets paid. But the Greek café was open, selling half-loaves of bread and bottles of milk and a few cigarettes to natives. He has dried wors on wire hooks and mebos in glass jars of syrup on the counter. If I have any money that's what I buy. Or sometimes a Sweetie Pie.

"Hey, Ken? We're way, way too early. We'll be there before seven. It only opens at eight!" But there could be others. Crowds of kids waiting. Then we'd be back of the line.

But my secret worry was really that other kids, bigger, tougher or just meaner, would get there just before the doors opened and push to the front. Or maybe that someone already there would say when we arrived, "I'm keeping places for my friends." A lot to worry about. My mom said, "Tell the man in the office if they push in." But she doesn't understand what a kid can do.

We went slower up the hill where we hardly ever rode. Just before the road went over the main railway tracks you could see the concrete headgears of Zandpan sticking up among the slimes dams. The Municipal Licence Office, with its grey corrugated roof and grey corrugated walls stood by itself in a field. There was a flattened piece of veld for cars to park and a steel bike rack. For some reason the building was not on the ground so steps led up to the door. At the top of the steps a small boy was looking down at us, smiling, with one hand on the door handle. Holding on tight. I knew what the kid felt. Dessington and I were bigger and meaner kids. The small kid was worried that we'd push to the front.

"How many licences are you getting?" I demanded.

"Just one. Just one. Just for me!" he said. And somehow all three of us knew it was settled.

The kid would get number one. I would get number two, Dessington number three. This kid was a way to make sure. We could protect ourselves if we protected him. Three people all shouting together. Other kids would have to push past all of us and we could make a huge fuss. But no one else came and at exactly eight o'clock a grey DKW car pulled off the road and parked. A huge man in a khaki safari suit huffed and puffed up the steps. While we pressed ourselves to the side, he unlocked the door, without even saying hello, went in and locked the door from the inside. All three of us groaned softly.

A few minutes later the door was unlocked and we moved into the small space in front of a wooden counter and wire grill. The man asked in Afrikaans who was first, and the small kid meekly raised his hand and said, "Me, Oom."

I saw that the licence the kid paid for was an orange square. It was my turn.

I looked down at the bike licence. It said number seven. I thought there was a mistake.

Without thinking I said, "It should be number two."

"The other one got number six. You get number seven." He looked over my shoulder at Dessington.

"My mother phoned last week, before New Year. You said we couldn't get them before today."

"They were booked by important people."

"It's not fair. I'm going to tell my father. He's friends of the mine manager at Hartebeesfontein!"

"Tell your father to call the police. Ha ha ha!" And then, "Maak dat jy wegkom." I waited outside for Dessington. He came out and just stared at me.

"I bet it was De Villiers or Morgan or one of the assistant mine managers for their kids," I said.

"Or Knott, or Solomon, or Crosby!"

We named most of the fathers in town who were above ours. There were enough kids with bikes to make it hopeless.

"I'm going to look at every bike in Stillies this year and find out."

"Me too. It's rubbish!"

"It's not fair!"

"It could be the police. A policeman's kid!"

"Or that hairyback took them for his kid and his friends' kids." Dessington hated Afrikaners. The mystery swept over us. It could be almost anyone.

"But there's five licences missing. It's a whole bunch of kids. Or different people were booking."

It was too complicated to work out.

"Well, at least we were the first there. We really got the number one and number two."

"No, we didn't! That small kid would have got number one."

We stopped at the park, laid our bikes on the ground and sat on the merry-go-round, slowly pushing ourselves around, trailing our shoes in the dusty rut. There were cars about now. Work had begun. It was getting hot.

"Want a cookie?"

He just stuck out his hand and asked, "I wonder why there weren't crowds of kids there?"

"Maybe they couldn't get up so early. Maybe they'll all be there this afternoon."

I looked at my licence. Bright orange with the number seven in the centre, a hole for mounting and "Bicycle Rywiel" painted around the edge. It was a good number anyway. I took out the bike spanner from the tough little leather pouch strapped behind the saddle. The bike spanner has different shapes and sizes cut out, so that you can take your whole bike apart and put it back together. Sometimes when we had nothing to do, we did that just for fun.

I loosened the wheel nut and put the new licence by itself on the right side.

I was happy. I knew we'd talk about it all year. We'd had a proper adventure. I'd got up early by myself and argued with a grown-up. I'd got the second-best licence except for the cheats and my plan had worked out. We'd been pretty brave.

Cattie

One Friday afternoon I was over at Dessington's making a kite. We split pieces of bamboo, tied the frame with cotton thread, glued the tissue paper with flour glue. Everything you have to do. It turned out okay but there was no wind so we left it on the floor of the garage.

His sister, Yolande, is always such a little nuisance. She was on the other side of the road in the Wheelers' driveway with a group of girls making a racket. Peter shouted at her to shut up and all the girls started sticking out their tongues and teasing, calling us stupid and ugly – stuff like that. So he got out his catapult and pretended to shoot at them, but they knew he was just pretending and started jumping up and down and daring us to really shoot.

That's when I fired a small stone high in the sky. They all looked up and when it came down it hit one of the girls in the face. She screamed and then they all screamed. She sat on the ground and the rest pointed at us. Then she lay on the ground. I saw blood on one of the girl's hands. Dessington was pointing at me and yelling, "It wasn't me! It wasn't me! *He* shot."

I jumped on my bike and raced home.

I put my bike in the garage and went straight to my bed-room, shut the door and slipped under the bed. I thought the best thing to do was hide. I knew the police were going to come. The kid was most probably in hospital already, fighting for her life. The phone would start ringing and first my mom and then my dad would start looking for me. Cars would fill our driveway. People would be knocking on the door. Her parents would be there, shouting and wanting to give me a hiding before the police arrested me. I didn't know how to escape or what to do. Every second seemed to take an hour.

I wondered how long I could last without eating. I looked at the springs under the mattress. There was fluff hanging there and also a feather, bluish-green, so it must have belonged to Freddie, my budgie, who died right above me on my pillow one afternoon, his thin legs sticking up in the air. He'd been sick for two days, sort of sitting on the bottom of his cage. I had the same feeling now. No hope that things would ever get back to normal.

I wondered which kid I had hit. It wasn't Brenda Wheeler or her sister, or Yolande. I can hardly remember most girls' names, even the ones in my class. Maybe she was just visiting in the hols. Maybe her parents were rushing now from some other town to see her before she died or before they had to operate or something. Maybe I'd blinded her. I was crying, but quietly.

Someone opened my door. Mom said, "Anybody home?" I heard her walk down the passage. She asked Ingrid if she'd seen me. Ingrid said she'd heard me come in, but didn't know where I was. My mother said, "Where does that boy get to?"

I lay dead still.

A car came up the drive. It was my dad; I knew the sound. A little later I heard him say, "Jean, I'm home." Now I knew William was putting the teapot on the tray with the cup and

37

milk and sugar and a plate of Marie biscuits or maybe a rusk. Dad would sit in his chair and smoke and read *The Star* and have cup after cup of tea. Then he'd go into the garden and walk everywhere, looking at everything, seeing if there was something to moan about. He'd even notice if I broke a small branch or stepped in a flowerbed.

When the phone started ringing he'd start yelling, I knew it.

The phone rang. Mom answered. She listened and spoke a bit. I couldn't hear what she was saying. Then she hung up. It was quiet again.

I must have dozed off because the phone woke me. She spoke again. She hung up and phoned someone. I couldn't stand it any more and got out from under the bed. I sat by my table and opened all my schoolbooks. I stared through the lace curtains into the garden and wished I was some other kid.

I heard my mom come down the passage. She stopped at my door and said, "Oh, there you are. Have you said hello to your father?" And then she walked away.

We had a normal dinner. I kept quiet. I ate the terrible cold mashed pumpkin without saying a thing. Mom and Dad spoke to each other most of the time. Dad said, "I'm going to turn in early tonight. I'm clapped out. Thank God it's the weekend." And that was that. Nothing happened.

Nothing happened the next day either. Every minute took an hour. Ingrid acted normal and I nearly made up my mind to tell her what had happened. The whole day I waited for the trouble to begin. All the stuff that was bound to be coming. Then I thought, maybe everyone's waiting for Monday. I wanted to phone Dessington but didn't; his mom or dad would answer and start shouting at me.

On Sunday I was beginning to think I'd imagined everything, but at the end of lunch, Dad, with a sort of empty look on his face, the sort of face a person makes when they are trying not to smile, asked, "Going to Peter's this afternoon?" I said, "No. I can't, it's Sunday."

"Oh," he said. "I forgot." But I knew they knew something.

A few weeks later when I was in the garden with my cattie, he said, "Careful where you point that thing." And that was that.

I stayed away from Dessington. He didn't phone or visit either. Later he told me that they took the girl to the dentist but there was nothing but a tiny chip. He said the girl's parents phoned his parents and his parents phoned mine. He wanted to know if I'd got strapped. I said he was a girlie girl and a tattletale.

I can't figure it out. Seeing as no one was badly hurt, Dad and Mom must have decided to let me off. The only thing is this: maybe my dad wants me to be rougher or something. Maybe he doesn't want to discourage me.

Kleilat

Six of us are pedalling fast, one behind the other. We're worried that someone's dad driving at the beginning or end of a shift will recognise us. We've finished school, had our lunch, and, as far as our mothers know, are playing at a friend's house. We guess it'll take an hour to get to the Vaal.

We're sworn to secrecy. Dessington, Allister Compton and his brother, Randall, me, and Peter and Barry Cornish. We're all in shorts, shirts and takkies. Only Peter Cornish wears a hat, a black cowboy hat with a gold band he got for his birthday. Some of us have catties wrapped around our handlebars and a few stones or marbles in our pockets.

Beyond the edge of the town, the side roads all have signs in English, Afrikaans and Fanagalo: *Mine Property. No Entry. Authorised Personnel Only.* A few natives, wrapped in blankets, are walking on a path towards the concession store.

I wish I could go underground and see how it works down there, but Dad says it's too dangerous and anyway we'd get in everybody's way.

We pass a row of bluegums planted as a windbreak when all this was just farmland. The white trunks glow under the dark tops, and when we pedal beyond them we can see the concrete headgears of Number One and Number Four shafts at Hartebeesfontein and a Buffels' headgear way to the south. A black-winged kite floats from a telephone pole and flies away into the empty sky.

In a mile or so we get close to a row of older houses hidden behind tall hedges at the entrance to the Buffelsfontein mine. This is a place where the gardens have had time to grow, and it makes me think of how it must be in England, and of William Brown, Ginger, Henry and Douglas hiding in the shrubberies as angry grown-ups search for them. Sometimes I think I'd like to live over there, in England.

We follow the road, and near the horizon I see a long line of dark green wandering through the veld. We are going downhill. The road is washed out in parts and is heading straight to the river. We speed up, then stop, one foot on the ground. A flat concrete bridge with no railings stretches across the sparkling water and a sign reads *Vaal Rivier. Vermaasdrift.* The banks are lined with trees but the river is low and there are big patches of sand and broken branches lying on the rocks and stones. On the far side lies the Orange Free State. It looks empty and sort of different.

There are two places kids can't ever go alone: the slimes dams, sloping up like pyramids behind the chain-link fences, with signs of skull and crossbones every few feet, and the Vaal River. We are here at last.

For weeks we've been planning for a real kleilat fight. Allister and I are the oldest and the team leaders. We spin a tickey and he gets to pick first: his brother, of course. I get Dessington, he gets Barry and I get Peter. We spin again for sides and I'm happy not to cross to the other side, where the police only speak Afrikaans and most probably hate kids from the Transvaal.

While they ride slowly across the bridge, we run down to

the river. The clicking of insects suddenly stops. I can hear and smell the river. Here we are! Far from grown-ups, our houses, the school, our streets. Deep in the bush.

We start cutting willow branches, testing them for whippiness, but they're too weak and we move to other trees looking for stiffer sticks.

Peter throws handfuls of water on the bank and mixes the sand to get the right stickiness of mud. That way, the ball of clay will stay stuck to the switch until the moment when it flies off, at the end of the cast. The river clay is black, not like the red soil everywhere else.

Dessington shouts, "I saw a fish jump! We should have brought a rod." Then he says, "I bet this place is full of mambas and scorpions!"

I laugh. "There's no mambas here. But I bet there are rinkhals and puff adders." I look across. "We better hurry! They're getting ready."

Our first tries are hopeless: the clay drops off behind us even before we throw. We squeeze more water out of the clay and begin to get the hang of the cast. Clay balls begin to land in the river. We can see that the others across the river are getting the feel of it too.

Allister is the first to get a shot clean across. There are shouts and cheers from the far bank. Then Peter gets one to fly at them perfectly and we yell too. I'm desperate to get one over because the team captain must. Most of our shots are splashing in the river, well short of the bank. I get one over and then another and feel really happy. Dessington nearly gets hit and acts as though he's dodged a bullet or a poisoned arrow or something. After a bit we realise that we are not going to hit one of them or they one of us and the game gets stale, and so, after shouting back and forth, the others ride back to our side and come down off the road to where we are.

Those with catties start shooting, trying to bounce pebbles across the river and onto the far bank. There are old weaver nests hanging over the river and I hit one, dead centre.

For a while we all move along the river finding things, turning things over, throwing things and calling everyone over to see things. We smell the pong of something dead.

Randall finds some tracks in the sand and whispers, "It could be a leopard!"

"It could be a sheep or a dog," someone says.

We're mine kids and don't have a clue. I don't say anything. "Let's swim! The water's warm."

"We don't have a towel."

"You could get swept away or towed under!"

"They'll see from our hair we were swimming." That thought stops us in our tracks.

"Maybe we should go now. We can't be late," someone says. We all sort of agree; Stillies is far away and we don't want to be caught. I put a few smooth river pebbles in my pocket and we climb up to the road and pick up our bikes.

Before Buffels we see a flock of guinea fowl run across the road in single file and disappear in the grass. Otherwise we just pedal and pedal with our heads down. A few cars and bakkies pass us but no one stops us or yells. As we get close to town, we begin to think we might have made it without being seen by anyone we know. We start laughing and making up stories about what we did.

Then Allister says, "If my father finds out he'll kill me and Randall! No one better tell!" He looks back at the Cornish boys: "They'll ask you to tell who you were with, then they'll call our parents. Never, ever tell them. If I get in trouble I'll donner you, I swear to God."

Peter says, "We won't tell. Why would we?"

The sun is low and it's getting cool. We're on the streets we know backwards. First Dessington peels off, then the Comptons. The Cornish brothers ride with me to my gate. They live just round the corner.

"Tell your mom we were playing Cowboys and Indians near those new houses over there," I point. "That's what I'm telling my mom if she asks."

And she did, just after she asked if I had any homework.

Now I'm lying in bed on my side, my one hand under the pillow, my eyes shut. The afternoon is spread out exactly as it happened. There are six of us out on the road pedalling fast.

Being Sick and Dying

Mom uses her nail polish to write a big, pink "K" on one of our plastic cups. That cup is for me and nobody else can use it. If they do, they'll catch scarlet fever too.

They take my door off the hinges and hang a wet sheet in the opening to keep my germs from getting out into the house. My throat is so sore I can hardly swallow, so Mom mashes my food into porridge and feeds me with a spoon like a baby.

Every term some kids get sick and pass it on and the school is nearly empty. One time it's whooping cough, the next time it's mumps or German measles or flu or chickenpox. The kids catch it from each other but this time I got sick by myself. No one else has got it and no one knows where it comes from.

The doctor whispers in the passage and my mom comes in and wipes my face with a wet cloth. I look through the lace curtains and dream of all the accidents on the Old Potch Road. The ones with donkey carts and burning Volkswagens and grown-ups crying. They push our heads down so we can't see, but this time I see all the bodies and birds flapping in the sky and I fall asleep. Mom says my nightmares come from the fever and she takes my temperature all the time. It goes on for weeks, I think, but maybe only days. I'm always hot and have to be helped to the bathroom but hardly anything comes out.

Dad comes in after work and says, "How're you feeling, my boy?"

I get better but then I catch measles and chickenpox together. Ingrid does too, so we share a room to keep each other company. We're like ghosts with all the calamine lotion. The curtains are kept drawn so we don't go blind and we listen to the radio and drink Kool-Aid and sleep. When it's all over the school term is finished and I'm so weak from lying down that Grandad Smith spends days helping me walk.

When I go back to school I tell my friends, "I could've died! Cross my heart. That's what the doctor told my parents. Ask them if you want. I'm lucky to be alive!"

When I first heard about dying I was small and I thought it meant everybody except me, then one day, suddenly, I knew it meant me too. Now I worry about it all the time.

That's why I hate that song "Who Killed Cock Robin?", and don't like *Babes in the Wood*, where the birds covered the bodies of the brother and sister with leaves. The children couldn't make it without grown-ups. It pretends to be just a fairy story but I know it's the truth.

I asked Mom if it hurt when you died and she said it was just like going to sleep except you didn't wake up here. She said you woke up in heaven but that seems like Father Christmas or the Easter Bunny – something grown-ups make up for kids.

A kid was taken to hospital late at night, a small kid I hardly knew, but we all knew his face. Mom said he was fighting for his life. Grown-ups were feeling their children's foreheads and asking them how they felt. Then Mom told us the kid had died and that we were never, ever allowed to play around piles of sand again. She went to the funeral and said it was

46

terrible. It was a disease that came out of the ground and it had a complicated name, meningitis something. It can kill you easily.

Then right after that, Robin Finney got cancer. He was sick for ages and used to sometimes come around with his folks and his brothers. All his hair had fallen out and he had a red handkerchief wrapped around his head, like a pirate. He scared me. He smiled a lot but had terrible headaches. I felt sorry for his brothers, who just sat quietly and looked at him and at their parents. Then they didn't come around for ages because he was too sick. We waited and waited and he died. There's no cure for brain cancer.

I think if it happened to me I wouldn't stop crying even when I was asleep. You know when something bad is going to happen and you wake up and just for a second you forget and then you remember and your stomach goes sick and you are stuck in your problem again. I think I'd cry until I died.

Matinee at the Rec

Stillies doesn't really have a centre, but the houses on the Stilfontein, Buffelsfontein and Hartebeesfontein side all slope down to the traffic circle where the two main roads meet. The Three Fountains Hotel, the post office and the playing fields are here, and so is the Strathvaal Recreation Centre, a huge white building that everyone calls "the Rec".

Every Wednesday and Saturday there's a bioscope matinee. I won't go on Saturday because it's too crowded and big kids push you around, but sometimes on Wednesdays my mom gives me a few shillings and says I should get out and do something different and I bike down.

The Rec is used for lots of stuff. There are talent shows, fancy dress contests, flower and vegetable competitions and meetings. My mom has won Best Barberton Daisy twice and also a prize for pewter work on a fancy-shaped wine bottle. We have the Mine Christmas Party here and every kid gets a present and a bag of sweets. There are pony rides around the cricket field and you can speak to Father Christmas and tell him what you want. There'd be hell to pay if you told a little kid that Father Christmas was really Mary Vivian's dad in disguise.

Last year the whole of Stilfontein came here to get the polio vaccine. It took all week but we went near the beginning because our surname begins with "D". The line went right round the parking area twice. The day we were there, the queue moved so slowly and it was so hot that kids started crying and fighting with their parents. "Don't stare!" whispered my mother and pointed her finger in another direction.

Sometimes Mom and Dad take us with them to see a film at night. We come here or go to Klerksdorp to the Leba Theatre. This year we've seen *The Nun's Story*, *Ice Cold in Alex*, *Tiger Bay* and *Ben-Hur*. And also *Carry On Nurse*. I always hope there will be an old black-and-white short film with Laurel and Hardy or Charlie Chaplin showing because it makes my dad laugh like crazy. When I peek, I see tears running down his face.

After locking my bike on the stands, I go into the foyer. You buy the ticket, sweets and cooldrinks at the same table. There is a poster of today's movie, *Comanche!*, on the wall. *They killed more white men than any other tribe in history!* is written on the side.

Next week's show is *Istanbul* with Errol Flynn. It's about a diamond thief, but it's really a love story, I can tell by looking at the picture.

I wander into the big hall with the other kids. The upstairs, with its slanted floor and comfy seats, is locked in the afternoons because kids are noisy and throw stuff down on the people below. But I sat up there with my whole family when my mom acted in *Dial M for Murder*. She showed Ingrid and me the trick scissors that she grabbed to stab the bad guy. It was welded to a hinge that they sewed inside his coat to make it look real. I was really scared when she was on the phone and he was hiding behind the curtain getting ready to kill her.

She loves amateur dramatics but Dad thinks acting is sissy

stuff, especially for men. The man who reviewed the play for the Klerksdorp paper said there were problems but my mom was very good. She called it "a decent crit" and pasted it in her scrapbook right below another one from the *Western Transvaal Record*. It read: "*The Hasty Heart:* Jean de Kok, as Sister Margaret, has never played better. Her performance was restrained and deeply moving. Her grace and deportment on the stage was a pleasure to watch."

I move from seat to seat until just before the lights go out so I have no one in front to block the screen. There are slide adverts for dry cleaners, movers with European supervision, butchers, stuff like that, and then a cartoon. *Beep Beep the Road Runner* is my favourite but I like *Tom and Jerry* as well. Next there's a Pathé newsreel with pictures the Russians took of the dark side of the moon from their satellite. They got to name all the craters and mountains on that side with Russian names because they saw it first.

After that they show the next episode of a serial about gangsters. I'm not sure what's going on but it ends at an exciting moment. My dad says they show serials to keep kids coming back, week after week.

During the interval we just stand around staring at each other. Some kids buy even more sweets and crisps.

The roll of the music at the beginning of the main film always gives me goose bumps. The lion roars or the guy beats the huge gong. Everybody says "Shish!" or "Shut up!" Then someone says "Shish!" one more time just to make people laugh.

Westerns are easily my favourite films. All my friends have

cap guns and holsters and we play Cowboys and Indians nearly every afternoon. When gunfighters come into the saloon and the cowboy pushes back his chair I wish I lived then. Or when the cavalry charge down the mountainside to rescue the people fighting inside the circle of wagons. Or when the good guys are drinking coffee around a campfire and someone hears a twig snap. I think some of the girls and even some of the squaws are beautiful but I don't tell anyone; they'd laugh themselves sick.

After the last shootout they slam open the big double doors at the back and the afternoon light streams in. I walk through the foyer not saying a word but I hope someone's watching me. My eyes move from side to side and my hands hover near my pants' pockets. I step outside and squint up at the sun and then, without looking back, walk slowly to my bike.

All the way home I'm in a gunfight.

The Hols

An icy cold wind blows here in winter. My dad says it was the same on the edge of the Sahara Desert during the war. Here it comes from the Kalahari and cuts right through our streets. Sand pings on the fly screens and stings our bare legs at school. Somehow it gets inside the house, so first thing every morning William has to dust.

Some grown-ups say the desert is spreading, but others blame the peanut farmers nearby for ploughing their fields at the end of summer and leaving the bare ground soil to be blown around.

On mornings when the birdbath freezes over, I lift the thin circle of ice and flip it onto the lawn. Mom puts gentian violet on the ulcers in my mouth and Vaseline on my split lips. Our noses are always running.

During the July holidays we drive to the South Coast to a rented cottage. Most people go at Christmas but we think the beaches are less crowded and the weather better in the winter. Mom says it's also way, way cheaper.

We drive at night because Dad can concentrate while we are asleep. The three of us lie in made-up beds at the back of the Opel station wagon, side by side, pushing and giggling until he warns us to be quiet or he'll turn around and scrap the whole bloody thing.

He and my mom sit in front talking softly and smoking. A box of Westminster 85s and a pack of Ransoms lie between them on the seat. Sometime late in the night he pulls off the road at the bottom of Van Reenen's Pass and wakes us. "Snow!" he says. And when we lift our heads he says, "Look at the snow!" The flakes fall quickly in the beam of the headlights, but somehow never get to the ground. It's the first time we kids have seen snow. We roll down the windows and put out our hands to feel the flakes and then stick out our tongues to try and taste them. We chatter as the car begins the climb upwards but then quickly fall back to sleep.

We play the same game every year as the sun comes up: First to See the Sea! Mom and Dad only pretend to play. I have the feeling they want me to lose, or at least for Ingrid to win for once. We start looking way too soon, maybe even twenty miles inland, and for ages, at every curve in the road, we strain to see the grey line of the sea between the hills of sugar cane or the Indian Ocean suddenly rising like a monster tidal wave.

And then it's there. Deep, dark blue and scary too.

"The South Coast" are almost my favourite words. The whole place is perfect. Lagoons filled with mullet, streams and green hills and small paths going up into the bush. Pondo women sit on the beach with their beads spread out on reed mats. Small boys by the road sell vegetable ivory, guavas, bananas, pieces of cane and live crayfish, hidden in baskets in the long grass. The shark nets offshore seem to rise and fall with the waves.

When we first unlock the cottage door the inside smells like salt and wet towels. It's small and everybody has to find a place to sleep. I sleep on the floor in the same room as

Uncle John and Dad. Mom sleeps with Ing and Gill. Gran and Aunty Toff share a room. At night after dinner we play Beetle or Happy Families or Snap. The radio is always on and Dad reads the newspapers. Now and then he says something like "Verwoerd's going to rig the election to get his bloody republic." Or "John, did you see this on Anglo American?" Or "Hell's bells! Thirty-eight people died in car crashes on the weekend! South Africans are definitely the worst drivers in the world." He likes a bowl of All-Bran before bed. Uncle John likes chocolates.

Mom and Toff sit planning the next days' meals and moaning about how difficult it is to make everyone happy.

Gran de Kok sits in the best armchair with a rug over her knees and chooses what programme we are going to listen to. She has her own box of crystallised ginger. We wait on her hand and foot but luckily I'm her favourite. She says to me, "Come here and sit with your old gran."

Spotty stinks of rotten bait and is tied up outside. Dad tried to wash him in the sea but got scratched and said to hell with it.

We love Ramsgate Beach. They say it's the safest beach, with no backwash or rip tides and it's protected from the wind. Every day we drive down after breakfast and stay until lunch. I walk through the parking area looking for TY, TX and TZ licence plates. That means people from Klerksdorp, Potch or Stilfontein. Or TOY, people from Orkney. Maybe people we even know, but in any case people from our part of the Transvaal. We keep count of those cars, all holiday long.

Every year, on one afternoon we drive down to Port Edward

and are pulled across the Umtamvuna River on the pontoon. Then Uncle John films the waves crashing on the rocks and we drive back again.

And on the last day before we leave, we have lunch at the Tea House of the Blue Lagoon. Everybody chooses what they like from the menu and then lots of us complain that we didn't get what we wanted.

Stilfontein is hours and hours away, somewhere up there in the middle of the veld. While I'm on holiday, I don't miss it a bit. I'd rather live here any day.

From the halfway mark of the holiday, I begin to count the days and feel sort of sick about going home. On one of the last afternoons while the grown-ups are napping, I sit on the rocks and try to fix what I see deep in my mind, like a photo, so I can keep it for ever.

A surfboat bounces through a wave and people wait on the sand. The wind smells salty. The beach curves to the far rocks. The clouds are smaller way out and I see smoke on the horizon. A tanker is going down the Wild Coast. The sea has the dark afternoon colour and the whitecaps shine far out to sea.

Books

At the end of the holidays, the week before school starts, every kid goes for a haircut. Mom says, "Make sure you tell them, 'short back and sides and top', otherwise it will be a waste of time and money." She gives me the exact change and tells me to take a book in case I have to wait: "You can't just sit and stare into space."

There's only one barber here and you hang around all morning or afternoon. It's so boring. You start in a queue outside the shop and slowly move inside, then you get a chair and move from chair to chair until it's your turn. I read a huge bit of a Hardy Boys while I wait.

Our house is so full of books that when kids come over to play they ask, "What are all these books for?" There are shelves all the way down the passage, stacks of books on bed-side tables, piles on the desk, boxfuls in the built-in cupboards. Dad says that when his ship comes in he'll turn a whole room into a library; in the meantime, he says, it's not too early for Ingrid and me to start our own.

Ingrid's bookshelf is full of ballet books, but she's also got all her annuals and her girl stories – *Little Women*, *Little Men*, *Jo's Boys*, *Fairy Tales from Turkey*, *Anne of Green Gables* – and her books of cut-out dolls. But her favourites are the ballet picture books, and her favourite of all of those is *Baron Encore*. Gill once scribbled in it with red and blue crayons, all over the photographs and everything, and Ingrid was so angry and cried so hard that her face and hair were wet. She nearly lost her breath and could hardly stop. Mom told her that Gill couldn't help it and that she shouldn't leave her books where Gill could find them.

Two painted circus cages that Uncle Jim made for me from sucker sticks keep the William books standing up on the top of my bookcase. I laugh so hard when I read them that I think I might explode. When they hear me, someone always says, "Ken must be reading a William." Each time a new one comes out, I get it for Christmas or my birthday.

I have Gerald Durrell's books, *Roberts Birds of South Africa*, *The Famous Five*, *The Secret Seven*, *Teddy Lester*, *Beau Geste*, my stamp album, some of Lawrence Green's books and TV Bulpin's books about Rhodesia and the Eastern Transvaal: *The Trail of the Copper King* and *Lost Trails of the Transvaal*.

Dad gave me all the annuals he got when he was a boy: *The Big Budget Book for Boys*, *Every Boy's Hobby Annual 1932*, *The Wonder Book of Inventions*. He makes sure I look after them, even though they are mine now and old and a bit boring. He also gave me all the copies of *Meccano Magazine* he saved. I read all the advertisements inside. When he was a boy, a Daisy pellet gun cost only six shillings and sixpence and a Dinky Toy double-decker bus cost fourpence.

He's got rules for books: one of them is don't eat while you read because you will get food on the cover or smear the pages. Mom does, though; she reads at lunch when he's not around. And one of the rules is the same as for his tools: "Put it back where you found it. Then the next person can find it."

He's always saying, "For heaven's sake, Ken, you've got to

learn to respect books. Never leave it like that, open and face down. Use a bookmark."

Once he caught me reading a paperback, a Jeeves book, in the bath, and yelled and yelled, "The moisture ruins the binding. Completely. I might as well throw it away now. If you do it again you can't borrow any of my books. Ever."

His own books are kept together by subject. He has a whole shelf on Napoleon (who he thinks is the greatest all-round person in history). Second is Churchill. If someone says something bad about him, Dad says, "All this debunking is ballyhooey. He saved us all. People have very short memories."

He has rows of books on South African history, brand-new books and books he finds in second-hand bookstores. General Smuts is also one of my dad's heroes.

He has a special bookcase where he keeps the most valuable books. It has glass doors to keep out the dust. Here he keeps the old book written by his grandad's brother, Karel de Kok. It's called *Empires of the Veld* and is a sort of history book about the Orange Free State. And then there's the Bible with wood covers given by Jan Smuts to all the people who fought in the war, his two red logbooks, his books on navigation and the big albums of his war photographs. There are also some poetry books given to him as school prizes: Keats, Shelley and Coleridge. He knows a whole bunch of them off by heart. He's even kept his exercise books from when he was at school; his handwriting is way better than mine.

On the normal shelves are hundreds and hundreds of orange Penguins. I read the spines: Jerome K Jerome, PG Wodehouse,

Aldous Huxley, *A Farewell to Arms*, *The Moon and Sixpence*, Graham Greene. And there are blue Pelicans too. It goes on and on.

If ever I say I'm bored or that there's nothing to do, he sort of smiles and says, "Read every book in the house, have you?"

Ingrid

When I tell Gilly that I'm the boss of the house, she says, "You're not! Daddy is. And that's flat."

If I say the same thing to Ingrid, she puts out her tongue and says, "You're only two years older than me. You can't be my boss. So whaa!"

I say, "I'm more than two years older. So whaa!"

Then Mom says, "Oh, tula, Kenneth! Go and do something. Read a book. Anything."

Ingrid is Dad's favourite. Sometimes he even sits and reads her poetry. She hardly ever does anything wrong and he never shouts at her. She's a goody-goody, but some days when it's raining and we have nothing else to do we'll play together. We invent games and get up to mischief, especially if little kids come to play with Gill.

We pretend that the built-in cupboard in my room hides a lift that goes underground; there's one floor where people make sweets and another where people make cakes. We tell her friends that we're the only ones allowed to fetch them. They get excited and beg us to go down. Ingrid tells me to go and get a little cake, one with hundreds and thousands on the icing, and pushes me into the cupboard. She stands in the room with the kids looking at the door and asks them if they can hear the motor. I stand inside trying not to laugh. After a bit I knock on the door and she lets me out. I have the cake in my hand. They look at me. "They are finished for the day," I say. "They only had one left for me." The kids start moaning and I break off small bits for each of them.

They ask me to go back and see if there are any sweets. Ingrid says we don't feel like any sweets today and they groan and say we're making it all up.

Actually Ingrid is pretty good at some things, like throwing and catching a tennis ball, and she's a fast runner. She's also the best person in the whole of Stillies with a hula-hoop. She hardly moves and it just goes up and up, right around her neck, then all the way down, then on one leg, then the other, then out on her arms. It's almost magic but I don't tell her. I just laugh and say, "I'm way better than you at the hula-hoop. You can ask anyone."

Once we poured tomato sauce, vinegar and sugar into a box and wrapped it in brown paper and string and put it out on the road. Then we hid behind the cedar hedge and watched the Klerksdorp bus stop dead and the driver get out and pick up the parcel. He looked at it on all sides. He shook it up and down, and listened. He got back on the bus. We laughed so much I thought we'd fall down.

The worst thing is, I'm afraid of the dark and I have to ask her to go down the passage with me and switch on my light. I think someone could be hiding and jump out and get me. She tries to hold my hand and after she puts on the light she waves her arms and says, "Look! Nothing!" I know she feels sorry for me, and even when she's furious she never tells my friends that I'm a scaredy-cat.

When we go back in the lounge Dad smiles and says, "Thanks, Ingy."

I always see shapes in the dark and hear noises outside. I lie awake listening. I peek through the curtains into the garden. I check under my bed and in the cupboards. I can tell just from looking if someone is dangerous. And I can see from faces if people are angry. Mom says I'm too sensitive. I know I'm a sissy and that Ingrid, Mom and Dad know. But Ingrid knows in a better way. She always wants to be friends with me, and if Dad is mean to me, I can see she feels sorry.

Also there's fibbing. I do, but she hardly ever does. Half the time, if I tell Mom or Dad something, they look at me for a moment, as though they're checking. Ingrid knows when I'm telling the truth, even when it sounds like a fib.

I wrote a real fairy story at school, like you read in a book. Two whole pages long, all about a princess. I showed it to Mom. She read it and said I couldn't have written it by my-self. She said I'd copied it from somewhere and shook her head and looked at me as though she was very sad.

I said I hadn't and she said, "Please, just stop. Stop fibbing. It's a terrible thing. Here, take this back." And she gave me my exercise book.

I sat on my bed and worried. I didn't know how to prove it was the truth. I'm a fibber, I know, but not this time. I thought up the story by myself. It took me two whole periods at school.

I couldn't go to Mr Chater, my teacher, and ask him to tell her. I let Ing read it. She said, "You could have written it. It's not that grown-up. Mom is being silly."

Some days, after school, Ingrid teaches her pretend class on the stoep. I lean against the wall and listen. She has small books for each kid and writes out their work and then corrects it as though she's the teacher. She calls each kid to the front of the pretend class and tells them what they did wrong. She even yells at the ones that made stupid mistakes or are causing trouble. I start laughing when she slaps them with a ruler and Mom sends me off to play somewhere else, even though I was first on the veranda.

Ingrid is mad about ballet. It's just about all she thinks about. She started lessons at the Rec, but now every week Mom takes her to Klerksdorp to Sylvia Franklin Ballet. When she comes home she has to show us all the little hops and pointy-toe things they do. She puts her hair in an Alice band like a proper ballerina, and wears a tutu around the house. Nadia Nerina and Margot Fonteyn are her favourites, and Mom even took her all the way to Johannesburg just to see Svet somebody-or-other dance at the Coliseum. That's where we all went to see *Around the World in Eighty Days*.

And she's always asking Grandad if he's sure he lost the old dance shoes that Anna Pavlova gave him when she danced in Joburg. We have a photo of him and his friends building the set for the theatre where she danced.

She walks through the house doing those spins and practising for the dance exams. She passes easily and can go to the Royal Ballet or Sadler's Wells, I'm not sure which, but luckily we don't have enough money. She's way too small to be by herself. Anyway, I suppose I'd miss her.

Cricket

On weekends in the summer, we'd be playing outside bare-foot. Ingrid doing the hula-hoop, hardly moving, Gill talking to herself and messing with blocks or dolls, and I'd be trying to catch a lizard in the hedge or practising headstands. Suddenly my dad would appear on the veranda shouting, "Hell's teeth, they got him!" and then go back inside before I could even ask him who or how.

He was saying one of our batsmen was out, but he wasn't really talking to us in the yard but to everyone in the world. It seemed he just had to do something with the bad news coming from the radio.

If South Africa got a wicket we'd hear him cheering at his desk.

He loved cricket more than any other game and played for Old Forestonians when he came back from the war.

After they started going out, my mom would go to his matches on the weekend and help with the scoring and the tea. When he asked her to marry him, he took her for a drive in his old Hillman and parked at a place with a nice view and said, "If I told you that all I own is this car and my cricket boots, would you marry me?"

Once I'd learned to catch a ball, he started teaching me how to hold a bat and how to grip the ball if I was bowling. He thought board games were boring, so cricket and hockey were the only games we played together. He'd come home from work and I'd hammer the stumps into the lawn near the thorn tree and wait for him. After a cup of tea, a quick read of the headlines and the Dagwood comic he'd walk out rolling up his sleeves and I'd ask him, "Do you want to bat or bowl?" He'd choose bowling so he could finish his smoke.

He'd make me play forward and he'd make me play off the back foot, again and again. I wouldn't hit hard because we'd lose the ball through the neighbour's fence, but if I pushed the ball down the gravel drive he'd say, "Good shot!"

I'd bowl leg spins and he'd show me how to use my wrist and vary the flight and warn me that if I wanted to be a spin bowler I'd better be ready to be "carted all over the place".

I could tell he wanted me to be a Springbok cricketer but we both knew there wasn't much chance.

Before they built the new houses my friends and I had our own pitch in the empty veld right across from our gate. We scraped off the weeds and grass and cut the rest as short as we could so we could field without getting our socks full of khakibos. Six or seven of us played after school and we'd always field for the other side and promise not to drop catches on purpose. Sometimes we'd even let Ingrid play.

As it got dark we'd rush to get in another few overs. There'd be arguments about whether someone was out or not, and sometimes one of the kids would walk home saying he'd never play with us again but he'd always come back.

I'd get a new ball at Christmas, not a Kookaburra but a good one, shiny, red and hard, but it soon got scratched and soft and the stitching started coming undone. We'd use it until it fell apart and then play with some old tennis ball.

From Standard Three on, I started playing school cricket. Mr Jones, the principal, coached us and we played on a proper mat that was nailed down in the middle of the school's playing field.

My dad used to come some afternoons to umpire and help out. He knew more about cricket than Jones, I could tell. Once he gave me not out when the wicketkeeper thought I was stumped and the next day two of the boys came up to me at school and said he was a cheat and only gave me not out because I was his son. I told them that my dad wouldn't do that, but they laughed and said he was a double cheat. I told him that night, but he just said they should learn to accept the umpire's decision and that was that.

We had matches against other schools. One Saturday we went to Orkney and played them on their playing field. My dad bought a pair of batting gloves as a prize for the best innings. I made 27 not out and he gave them to me and no one complained. In the car on the way home he said, "That was a nice knock!"

One summer, a team from Anglovaal head office came down from Johannesburg to play Hartebeesfontein Mine. I sat on the grass down at the Rec the whole morning and afternoon, watching. Dad was the mine's captain and scored most of our runs and took a pile of wickets, but we still lost. When I said I was sorry, he smiled and said he was way past his best.

In 1956 he took me to my first Test match at the new ground at The Wanderers. On Christmas Day I was more excited about what it would be like to go just with him on

Boxing Day than about getting presents and having the big family lunch.

The Springboks were playing the MCC and we had tickets for the section in front of the change rooms where you could sit on the grass and watch the teams from close up. We went early to get a good spot and walked with a mass of people down Corlett Drive carrying our cushions and lunch. The place was already packed with more people than I'd seen in my whole life.

Just standing there with him before the start of play, I could see Denis Compton, Jim Laker, Trevor Goddard, Hugh Tayfield, Neil Adcock and Johnny Waite walking around and chatting like normal people. Some of the players even came out to the fence and gave autographs and I got Russell Endean to sign his name on our programme. Once the match started Dad told me to stop chattering and concentrate.

There were open stands, one big covered stand and two special stands for Indians and natives that faced into the afternoon sun. They always cheered for the foreign team. My dad said that it was a way to show that they didn't like our government. I thought it was scary and brave at the same time.

At morning tea the groundsmen roped off the pitch and people came onto the field and tried to decide whether it was breaking up or would take spin but all I could see was thin grass. Hundreds of kids and some grown-ups played stick cricket all over the field and had to be told to get back to their seats before the fielding team came out again. Dad bought me a Coke at lunch and late in the afternoon he had a beer and got me an ice cream.

He thought most spectators didn't know much about the game, but he started talking to a man who remembered players from when he was a boy. They decided which cricketers from long ago were the best: Don Bradman, Wally Hammond, Bruce Mitchell and lots of others. And they spoke about great matches they had seen before the war. They decided who was the best googly bowler and who'd hit the best cover drive they'd ever seen, and who'd taken the greatest catch.

They both thought Adcock and Heine were the best opening fast bowlers we'd ever had.

I listened to them as the bowler began his run and the field moved in. Everything went quiet. You could hear pigeons cooing on the golf course and then the click of the ball hitting the bat and a long sigh and everybody started talking again. The sun was going down behind us and we were sitting in the shadow. I had my arms around my legs and my chin resting on my knees.

Uncle Jim

Mom stood with both hands on the gate at 143 Van Riebeeck and called "Jimmy! Jimmy!" She moved down the fence and called again. It was the middle of the afternoon and dead quiet. I could see through the windows and empty rooms of our old house, right through to the veld on the other side. The house looked hollow, but she still thought he could be hiding there.

"Why don't you go and knock? Maybe he can't hear you," I said.

"Please be quiet, Kenneth! Please!" She took her cigarettes from her apron pocket. "Stay right here. I'm going to ask Mrs Pemberthy something."

She crossed the road and even before she got inside the yard her friend's front door opened. They stood and talked.

My mom's brother, my Uncle Jim, causes us a lot of trouble. He's divorced and drinks all the time. My dad got him work on the mine as a fitter, but soon after he started he got fired, was kicked out of the Single Quarters and came to live with us. He's nice but he stares right at you and frightens me a bit. He's bigger than my dad.

We'd moved from number 143 Van Riebeeck to number 156 because of my dad's promotion even though my mom wanted to stay put. She said, "Ten times in ten years is more than enough!" She didn't want to sew new curtains or transplant her Barberton daisies or pack everything into boxes and then unpack them all over again.

Anyway, Uncle Jim helped us move and then he just disappeared, leaving most of his stuff lying on the floor of the spare room. My friend Allister said that his dad said that Uncle Jim had stolen from the mine and that the police were going to catch him. I said his dad was a liar and I'd get my dad to fire his dad.

My mom came back. "I'm so, so furious with Uncle Jimmy. This is the last time. I'm finished and klaar." I saw her blinking her eyes. We walked together to our new house.

That night she told Ingrid and me not to answer the phone at all, and my dad had an argument with someone who came to the front door looking for Uncle Jim. I heard Dad say, "Do me a favour, stay off this property and tell the others that the same goes for them." It was scary.

After that things became normal. We weren't sure where he'd gone, and anyway they didn't talk about it in front of us. Mom invited his wife and our cousins to visit in the holidays. She felt terribly sorry for them, and even though it wasn't her fault, she said she felt somehow responsible.

One Saturday more than a year after he left, we drove to a farm near Potch to see a man who'd been helping Uncle Jim. On the way, Mom told us that he'd been living and working there and that he'd done really well. We were going to have tea and we'd better remember our manners. The gravel road had grass down the middle and when we got to the top of a hill I could see dark green trees on both sides of the river.

The walls of the farmhouse were whitewashed and low like a rondavel and the roof was rusty brown. All around were kraals made of twisted thorn wood. A windmill was squeaking near the dam and there was a concrete tank covered with green scum.

"Phew!" I said. "Smell that!"

My dad turned around to look at me. "If you say one thing like that in front of these people, I'll –", but he didn't finish because a man with a bad limp had come out of the house and was hobbling towards us. He took off his hat and said, "You must be Jean. You look like your brother."

"Mr Pienaar, I am so pleased to finally meet you. We have spoken so often on the phone, I feel like we are old friends. I'm so grateful for everything you've done." She held his hand.

"Please call me De Wet. We are old friends."

"Oh, thank you! This is my husband, Steffen. And our children, Kenneth and Ingrid."

Mrs Pienaar came out of the house and all of us were introduced again. She spoke no English and my dad tried to talk Afrikaans but couldn't.

We went into the house and both my mom and dad said how lovely it was. I looked at a stuffed kiewietjie on the kist and the horns of a blesbok on the wall. And then we all sat down and waited for tea and coffee, but luckily Mr Pienaar said Ingrid and I could look around the farm if we wanted.

We ran to the dam and saw turtles sleeping on a rock and bubbles coming up between the water lilies. I bet Ingrid that the dam was full of fish. We looked for the pig that Mr Pienaar said was bigger than a cow but couldn't find it. The kraals were full of muck and cattle and there were flies everywhere.

It was hours and very nearly dark before we said goodbye. Mom was so happy. She said that De Wet thought Uncle Jim was the best worker he'd ever had. He was helping others with their drinking problems, he went to church every week, he went to Alcoholics Anonymous meetings and he hadn't had a drop to drink for a year. Best of all, he had decided to come on holiday with us and "patch things up" with Granny and Grandad.

My stomach felt funny. I rested my arms on the open window and watched the sun slanting across the grass. We drove through a stream and I heard the hissing sound of the tyres in the water.

A week later, just as we were sitting down for dinner, Uncle Jim showed up. He was wearing a brown suit and a white shirt and his shoes and suitcase were dusty. I guessed he must have hitchhiked from somewhere. He was sunburned like the men who stand on the side of the road with their thumbs out. I'd forgotten his blue, blue eyes and his black moustache.

"Hello, Jeannie." He kissed her and then said, "Hello, Stef." He looked a little shy. He pretended to stare at me and said, "You're growing like a weed, sport."

He kissed Ingrid on the cheek and said, "Hello, sweetie."

My dad said, "You're looking fit, Jim."

Gill said, "Hello, Uncle Jimmy."

He put his case on the floor and knelt to open it. Right on top was something wrapped in damp newspaper. "From De Wet," he said. "Asparagus crowns. I'll make an asparagus bed before we go to Ramsgate."

It was still dark when I closed the gate and waved to William standing on the stoep with Spotty. Dad said, "We're off. Settle down, it's going to be a long day." He lit a cigarette and we started driving. Uncle Jim was sitting in the front with him. My mom had gone by bus to Johannesburg with Gill the day before and was driving to Ramsgate with Granny and Grandad. They'd be there before us. Grandad was going to teach me to fish off the rocks and how to tie live bait on the hook.

Once or twice in the morning Uncle Jim offered to drive but Dad said he was fine. They didn't talk much. Uncle Jim tried, but my dad hardly ever just chats.

We stopped for early lunch at a lay-by between Standerton and Volksrust. Mom had packed sandwiches for us the day before. There was a thermos of tea but Ingrid and I drank purple Kool-Aid. Cars roared past and then all of a sudden all you could hear was quietness and insects chirping in the grass. Dad said he was going to stop in Harrismith for petrol and if anyone needed to go, that was the time.

The main street through the town was steep and that meant the mountains were beginning. We pulled into a Caltex station. It had a sign saying *Clean Toilets*. Ingrid and I went while my dad filled up and checked the oil; then he went. Uncle Jim came from the café with crisps and a Coke for everyone.

"Tell your dad I'll be back in a second." He ran across to a brick building on the corner. The sign read *New Central Hotel*.

Dad came back to the car and asked where Uncle Jim was. I pointed. My dad said, "Jesus!" and put his head down but Uncle Jim came out of the hotel right away and crossed the road.

"Sorry Stef! Had to go. Knew you were in there."

73

The car filled up with the sour, grown-up smell of drink. Uncle Jim started eating crisps. Dad became dead quiet. I had the sick feeling I get when grown-ups cry or fight. They hardly spoke, and after a bit Uncle Jim slept with his head against the window right over Van Reenen's Pass and halfway to Pietermaritzburg.

In the late afternoon, I saw the sign for Amanzimtoti and knew we were close to the sea. I looked at Ingrid. I wanted to play First to See the Sea! but didn't know what to say.

"How much longer, Dad?"

"About an hour. Not long." I looked for the sea by myself.

We crossed the long, open bridge to Port Shepstone. Down below was the lagoon and the estuary. Some kids were playing on the small beach, but there was no sea to swim in, just rock pools and crashing waves. Nobody came here for holidays. The town was only busy on rainy days and Saturdays when grown-ups drove from their hotels or cottages to hunt for bargains in the Indian shops.

Uncle Jim suddenly spoke. He sounded hoarse. "Sorry to spring this on you, Stef, but I want to look up an old friend who lives around here. Drop me off anywhere. I'll come down to the cottage first thing in the morning. Or maybe even this evening if he's not around."

My dad slowed down but kept driving. "My God, Jim, your dad's waiting! He hasn't seen you for years! Your mother. Everyone's expecting you."

"Not now, Steffen! I want to get out!"

He looked at my dad as though he would fight. I was scared stiff. I looked at Ingrid; she was scared too.

My dad pulled over. He looked straight down the road and said, "Please, Jim."

Uncle Jim turned around and looked at Ingrid and me. "Have the first swim for me, okay?" We just nodded.

"Thanks for the drive, Stef. See you tomorrow." He climbed out and went to the boot and lifted out his stuff. He winked at me through the back window, turned and walked back the way we'd come. I watched him. He didn't ask for directions or look around or wave or anything. He just swung his suitcase as though everything was normal.

That was the last time I ever saw him.

My dad whispered, "It was impossible to stop him," and he put the car in gear.

The last few miles are the best. You go through small sea-side towns separated by miles of rocky bush and each one has its own special beach. Usually I would count from Shelly Beach on: St Michaels-on-Sea, Uvongo, Margate, Baven-on-Sea and then Ramsgate. But this time I couldn't get excited even though I wanted to. Whatever I said would seem wrong. Whatever I said would make Dad cross. Now and then Ing and I looked at each other.

We found the cottage after a few wrong turns. It was on the Southbroom side of Ramsgate and was sitting right above the rocks. Grandad's Morris Oxford was parked on the grass. Mom came quickly out of the back door and walked towards us, smiling. My dad said, "Just stay inside here a minute." He got out and she hugged him like she always did. He whispered to her and she put her head on his shoulder. After a bit we got out and she kissed us and asked us if we were okay.

Gran and Grandad were sitting inside and Gran said, "Oh no" and started crying. My dad said, "I'm sorry, Mrs Smith, I couldn't stop him."

Grandad looked up. "No one can. He does what he wants and the rest of us can go to hell." He went on winding line from a spool onto his reel.

The next day everyone was hoping like mad he'd come, but no one said anything. We also knew he wasn't coming. When we went down to the beach, Gran stayed at the cottage. In case.

Near the end of the holiday my dad and I waited with a small group for the skiffs to come in. They watched beyond the waves for the right moment and then raced together between the swells, caught up with a wave, cut their motors and were carried close to the shore. Men ran into the water right up to their shirts and dragged the boats up the beach.

Red roman, kob, geelbek and a barracuda were put on a sheet of plastic. My dad tried to bargain but quickly decided to buy the back half of the barracuda. He held it by the tailfin and lifted it on his shoulder. We waded barefoot across the Little Billy River and walked back towards the cottage on the hard wet sand. The sun was already behind the hills and the long beach was in shadow, but the sea was still sparkling.

We climbed up the path through the grass and rocks to the stoep. Gran was sitting there peeling fruit, a newspaper across her lap. "That's a lovely piece of fish, Stef. I'll fry some for dinner tonight and curry the rest."

I sat down beside her and she gave me a piece of guava

balanced on the blade of her knife, and then a piece of pine-apple. She waved towards the beach and the sea. "Just look at that, Ken! It's as pretty as a picture."

Sundays

Mom and us children are Methodists, but Dad's an agnostic or something and only goes to church on Christmas Day or for a funeral. But he was also sent to Sunday school when he was a boy, and to prove it he showed me the two books he won as prizes. Inside it says "La Rochelle, Wesleyan Methodist Sunday School". One book is for 1928 and the other for 1929. Once I heard him say that religion is pure superstition, but he lets Mom say what she wants about church and Jesus without interrupting. We take it in turns to say grace and he closes his eyes and pretends, otherwise Gill gets mad.

If Mormons or Jehovah's Witnesses come to our house, my mom or Gran invites them in and listens to what they have to say, but Dad thinks it just encourages them.

They start coming all the time; some Saturday mornings we see whole families walking up the drive. My dad says, "Oh hell!" and goes out the kitchen door. The visitors sit on the couch and have tea and discuss stuff and then everyone prays. I think they have nowhere else to go. For ages, two Americans from Salt Lake City came. Mom warned them she wouldn't be converted, but she says they're sweet boys, far from home and always welcome as far as she's concerned.

Every Sunday we go to Sunday school. It's almost impossible to get out of it. If you say you're sick, Mom makes you spend the whole day in bed. "You said you were sick, you can't suddenly be better now that we're back from church."

Mom makes me dress like I'm going to school: shirt, shorts and socks and my good shoes. Ingrid wears her best dress and gloves and carries a stupid little handbag.

There's hardly any traffic, the shops are shut and it's quiet. Everybody's inside except for people driving to church and servants in their best clothes walking around on their day off. When we get to the new church on Selborne Road, cars line the side streets and even the pavements. Except for the headgears, the church steeple is the highest point in Stillies.

We go into the Sunday school room at the back and the grown-ups go into the church.

The Sunday school teachers pretend it's not like school but it's even more boring and there's always an older girl, in training, trying her hardest to be the strictest. They tell us where to sit and what to do for the whole hour. The main thing is reading stories from the Bible. Then they ask us what we think the story means, but we're always wrong. It always means something different. And the Bible doesn't have a proper ending so it's never finished. Sometimes I nearly fall asleep and my head jerks up. You hear the minister's sermon coming in from the church or the sudden sound of the piano just before they start singing.

When we stand and sing I hear my own voice and it's never the same as others, so I just move my lips and pretend.

We get a cardboard stamp that has a Bible picture and text each time we go. When you have four of those you get a bigger one. Then four big ones and you get an even bigger one. When you have three of those you get the giant one. So if you go all year you get the giant one that's got something fancy around the edge. This rewards good attendance, Mom says, and she bought us each a notebook where we glue in the stamps, but I don't think any kid would go if they weren't forced to.

I'm sometimes chosen to hand out the stamps, and I keep a few extra ones. And then I get a bigger one, and so on, so that, even though we always go together, I have lots more stamps than Ingrid.

I flip through my book and say, "I'm beating you hollow!" She gets furious and says I'm just a stealer and a cheat and she's going to tell Mom, but she never does. She also thinks I steal money from the collection plate because I rattle the coins when I put in my tickey, but that's a big fib.

Just before Christmas, the Sunday school puts on a Nativity play for the church at the night service. Last year they dressed me up as a shepherd in my striped dressing gown with a towel over my head and a fake beard stuck on my face. I watched the flock and then stood in the manger with the Wise Men, while everyone sang "We Three Kings". Someone brought a real sheep to make it look real and I was hoping it would poo but it didn't. Just thinking about it, I nearly burst out laughing. If someone had noticed, they might have thought I was crying.

Harvest Festival is another special Sunday when kids are allowed in the church. I look at all the bread and pumpkins and watermelons and mielies stacked on the window ledges and trestle tables and wonder how they find the poor people to give the stuff to.

The sermon is always about the same thing: how to be good

and what you have to do. I keep paging through the Methodist hymn book looking to see who lived longer than Charles Wesley. He lived from 1707 to 1788, so that makes eighty-one years. Mary Duncan lived for only twenty-six years. So far she's the unluckiest. William Henry Parker lived from 1845 to 1929 – that's eighty-four. Jemima Luke lived for ninety-three years. I once found someone who made it to ninety-seven, but now I can't remember the page number. Mom whispers to me to stop fidgeting and then takes the book from me and puts it on the shelf on the back of the pew in front of us.

Every few years there's a terrible drought, the dams are empty and the mielies die. Ministers from all the different religions pick a Sunday to pray for rain. Then if there's no rain, we pray again the next week. If it rains, they say it's proof God is looking after South Africa. If it doesn't, it means we've done something wrong. Dad says that God's most probably got a few other things to worry about and then he laughs.

After their service, Gran and Mom stand around and talk for ages. Everyone crowds about, but especially around the Reverend Welsh, who Mom thinks is a saint. He once said that Gillian was sent by God to test our family but I think that's rubbish. People are so dressed up and the children have to stand around being perfect. The car is boiling hot and I just want to go home, get changed and do something like have a sandwich and get barefoot. I'd even sit quietly in the lounge doing nothing rather than be here, waiting.

On Sunday afternoons my mom and dad always have a nap. Sometimes they even lock their bedroom door. We have to be quiet for hours, so we play in the garden or just stand at the gate and stare at the veld. Nobody goes anywhere.

Mom says it's not healthy to have a bath on a full stomach, so late in the afternoon all of us bathe so we're clean for school on Monday. She always pours a lid of Dettol in the water. It goes milky then disappears. She says it kills germs. I used to bathe with Ingrid but Mom says we're getting too big. For dinner we have toasted sandwiches or bacon and eggs. She hates making supper on William's day off.

She comes to tuck me in and kiss me good night and asks if I've said my prayers. I tell her I'm going to. I don't kneel but lie in bed with my arms flat against my sides and my eyes closed. I pray because if I don't someone in the family might get sick or die. I pray for Spotty too, because he could get lost or run over by a car.

The Yard

The jackie hangman sits on the fence near the gate. It's black and white like a waiter and never stops twitching. I creep closer and raise my pellet gun. Slowly, slowly, because the bird always manages to fly away just before I shoot. It flies away this time too and doesn't land close, so I give up. Of all the birds around here, this is the one I want to shoot the most. It seems to tease me.

I hunt in my yard from one end to the other. I've stopped shooting mossies and wagtails because they're too easy, but I go after mousebirds and bulbuls because they eat the fruit. I once got a red bishop bird flying overhead. It was an incredible shot, but I couldn't tell anyone. When I picked it up, a bubble of blood came from its beak and its head lolled over my finger.

From the front gate you can see right across the Old Potch Road. The veld runs all the way to a clump of wag-'n-bietjies on the horizon. Sometimes we see farm natives riding horses up there, and once they suddenly turned and galloped towards Dessington and me when we were hunting for meerkats. We ran like crazy, climbed through the barbed-wire fence and ran across the road to safety.

Yesterday, after lunch, someone shouted that a veld fire was coming towards us. It'd been burning all morning over on the Klerksdorp side and had jumped the road. Mom, Ing and me, William and the ironing girl, all of us ran out. The

83

neighbours were beating the burning grass with sacks and wet towels to save their hedges and lawns. Smoke made our eyes water and insects were flying up and birds diving down to catch them. We were winning and the fire was almost out when I picked up a rock to drop on a bush of burning khakibos. I'd forgotten that fire had been burning around the rock. I screamed so loudly that people thought I'd been bitten by a snake or something. Mom told me not to make such a fuss and took me inside to put butter on the blisters.

Today is boiling hot and huge black clouds are in the sky. Dust devils are spinning grass ash down the drive and across the yard. Mom is worried that the washing will get dirty and sends William outside to take it off the clothesline and bring it in. I pray it doesn't rain because tonight Dad's going to show us Sputnik.

For weeks during the six o'clock news, Springbok Radio plays the four beeps of Sputnik's signal. Our teacher says it proves the Russians want to take over the world.

We stand together looking up at the sky over the garage roof, and one by one we all see it. A tiny star, moving slowly past all the others. Dad says it's flying at thousands of miles an hour and going round the whole world every hour and a half. I ask him if we can stay up and watch it come around again, but he says it's already way past our bedtime.

From our other gate, on Plettenberg Drive, you see the road curve and houses on both sides, most with green tiled roofs. Everybody has the same type of fence but each yard is different. Some have flowerbeds and bushes, others have no grass and broken toys lying about. Mom says that in some of these houses the children are "very neglected". The small ones have runny noses and are always crying and the older ones stare at you.

This is the side where the donkey carts stop to sell mielies, watermelons and yellow peaches. Spotty runs to the gate and keeps jumping and barking until whoever is standing outside goes away. Natives come to the gate and call "Baas! Baas!" or "Madam! Madam!" and sometimes Mom sends me out with a sandwich and tells me to say sorry, but she has no work for them.

You can't be sure which side the ice-cream boys will pass on their bikes, so you have to be listening for their bell and run to stop them and ask them to wait and then run inside to beg for money from Mom. Sometimes they even sell me a small piece of dry ice for experiments.

When Nichols & Coleman were building these houses, they were told to leave as many of the veld trees as they could, so our yard has two big thorn trees that have yellow flowers in spring and a clump of wild bushes that Dad says I must stop using as my fort. We've planted a grapevine, peaches and a plum tree on the Plettenberg side and a willow and evergreen trees on the other. They're still small and I wonder what they will look like when they're huge. We're always watering the garden because it hardly ever rains. Dad comes home and says, "Did anyone remember to water?"

The driveway is made of brown stones and gravel, and if you pedal at full speed and use the back brake you can make a skid mark for miles. The first day I got my bike I did it again and again until I fell and cut my knee and elbow, but Mom was only worried about the dented bell. She said Dad would be furious.

When I'm big I'm going to be a game ranger or maybe a zoologist. *Jock of the Bushveld* and *Memories of a Game Ranger* gave me the idea. But so did *My Family and Other Animals*. It's almost my favourite book. Gerald Durrell was the luckiest kid in the world.

Already I know heaps. Even Dad says I know a lot about animals, but he says I still better be good at arithmetic. I don't know why.

I can sometimes tell by the way a bird flies into a bush whether there's a nest in there. I collect eggs and keep them in a wooden box divided up into small squares. The egg lies on cotton wool and each square is labelled with a piece of paper with the name of the bird. I take only one egg from the nest and make tiny holes on both ends and blow out the yolk stuff. I've got doves, rock pigeons, mossies, weavers, bulbuls and mousebirds. Even a hoopoe. I found the hoopoe nest in a hole in a tree and fished the egg out with a bent spoon.

I trap birds so I can look at them close up. My wip is near the aviary because wild birds are always looking for seeds the doves have scattered from the cage, and I sit with the string in my hand outside the back door. This one time a whole flock of tiny birds landed and hopped about tweeting. I'd never seen them before and I felt my heart beating and my hand shaking. I prayed they'd hop under the chicken wire and pulled the string taut, ready to go. One hopped under, then hopped out again. Some mossies landed all together and the small strange birds flew off, but then they came back. All the birds were hopping around pecking at seeds: a mossie went under, then two or three of the others. I pulled the string and got them all, fluttering under the wip. I slipped a piece of tin along the ground and had them. I carried the lot into the aviary and ran off to get the *Roberts Birds of South Africa*.

They were black-cheeked waxbills. Prettier even than Uncle Dick's roller canaries, and I freed them in the aviary so I could show Dad when he came home. He looked at them for a bit and said I should get them out of there quickly because they might carry some disease and kill the doves. I waited until it was dark and went in there with a torch and caught them one by one, and let them go.

Murder

When we first lived at the top of Van Riebeeck, at 143 and then at 156, we were right at the edge of the town. The road just made a curve and became Gamtoos. Beyond the last house was just veld, the dead-end where Van Riebeeck would one day be extended, and the Old Potch Road. The sun set there. We made the cricket pitch and hunted and explored and crossed the road when no one was looking.

All the mines were doing well. More people were needed and the mine decided they had to build more houses. The builders started clearing the veld and digging for the water pipes. I hated it. They took away our special playground.

They dug up the ground for foundations and scraped the veld for roads. There were big piles of red sand everywhere. Some houses were nearly finished and they were just starting on others; one had string lines and cement and a few bricks and the next had finished walls. Another had rafters and stacks of green tiles on the ground. The foremen watched the natives spreading soil for grass and putting up the wire fences and gates. All day long you could hear the sound of cement mixers, and every afternoon after school we'd go up there and run through the empty houses and play on the piles of sand after the grown-ups had gone home. We'd run and slide and throw clods at one another.

Then they stopped us from going there ever again because a kid died of meningitis.

At breakfast one morning just before Christmas, my dad was listening to the news on the radio. I heard the radio say "In Stilfontein …"

He said, "Good God!" and called, "Jean! Come and listen to this." They listened and only then remembered to tell us to go and brush our teeth. But by then I knew a policeman had been murdered right outside, in the empty veld where the new houses were being built.

It happened in the middle of the night. His body was lying half outside his bakkie with a bullet right through his heart. Policemen were coming from all over the Transvaal to catch the murderers. They said it was a gang of thieves stealing building materials, and then they said it was a madman or probably a native. No one knew. Someone said a gun was lying on the ground, and then someone else said his gun was stolen. He had tried to radio the police station as he was dying saying, "Hello! Hello!" Or maybe, "Help! Help!"

Dad said it was nonsense, that nobody with a bullet in his heart would use the radio.

That's all anybody talked about at home, at school and in the shops. It was on the radio all the time and even in the big newspapers from Joburg, *The Star* and the *Sunday Times*.

They arrested all the natives who didn't have passes and made them talk. Then they came to the houses nearby and asked us what we'd seen the day before it happened. No one knew anything. Every time a new story started, Dad said we shouldn't listen to rumours.

The whole town was scared. Grown-ups locked the doors and wouldn't let kids play outside their own yards or ride their bikes to the shops. Dad said Spotty would bark if someone knocked on the front door and I was glad.

Then they caught him. He was the son of a lady who lived next door to the Wagners on De Mist Avenue. He'd been in jail in the Orange Free State for stealing or something like that and had escaped because he wanted to spend Christmas with his mom. Somehow the policeman had seen him hiding in one of the new houses and tried to arrest him.

My dad said, "He doesn't have a hope in hell. They'll hang him in Pretoria Central for sure."

Everything went back to normal, except that we're famous now. Everyone, all over South Africa, knows that Stilfontein is the place where a policeman was murdered.

Monday the Eleventh

This morning Granny Smith phoned and said we'd better come quick because Grandad was getting sicker. He'd had his gall bladder taken out a few days ago and something has gone wrong.

Dad called school and told them Ing and I wouldn't be coming and we all piled in the Consul.

It's one hundred miles to Joburg and, unless there's roadworks or an accident, it takes two hours. I get carsick if I read, so even though I've brought *Darkie & Co* in case, I look out the window and tick off my markers.

The first is just outside town, opposite the huge slimes dam. This is where John Astrup and I wait on our bikes on Saturday mornings for the Wall's Ice Cream truck to come from Potch. We hear the chimes long before we see it. I buy an orange Popsicle, but he's an only child and buys a packet full of stuff and then races home to put it in the freezer section.

The next marker is a bit further on, near the new golf course. Last year a flock of mousebirds hit our windscreen there and Dad had to get out and wipe the blood off with tissues.

Mom is going to have a baby in three weeks and has stopped smoking, but she's started again and is dead quiet, resting her head on the window and looking away. I know she's scared. It makes me scared too. She's Grandad's favourite and once told me that he loved her more than anyone else in the world. She said, "I don't know why, but my dad thinks I'm perfect." For ages I've wanted to tell her I do too, but I don't know how to say it.

There's only two turns to get through Potchefstroom, but I always get them mixed up. On one corner is a fish and chip shop, and sometimes we pick up lunch or dinner on our way through. Everything's wrapped in newspaper and smells of vinegar and Mom pops chips into Dad's mouth as we drive along.

Potch has a drive-in and just after it opened Mom and Dad brought us here as a surprise. We had no idea where we were going, and they wouldn't tell us even though we were over-excited. Once we got there we took ages to get comfortable. We sat on pillows on the back seat so we could see the screen. Then there were a few drops of rain as we waited for it to get dark, but it stopped and we watched the whole of *Friendly Persuasion*. It was about the American Civil War and the Quakers.

For ages after Potch there's only veld and hidden farm-houses. You only know they're there by the bluegums and the windmills. The mielies have been harvested but the stalks are still sticking up and I look down each row as we whizz by and I can tell we're going fast. I play the car war game. If anyone comes up close behind, I line up the small white triangle on the back window with the car's bonnet and blast them to smithereens. I'm a Spitfire; they're a Stuka.

Suddenly my dad says, "Ken, can you please stop talking so much?" I didn't even think I'd been saying anything. I look at everybody but they say nothing.

On top of one high koppie is the Theron Monument,

shaped like the trigger of a Martini-Henry rifle. Every time we pass by, Dad tells the same story. Danie Theron was a simple schoolteacher who became a scout and got shot up there by the British in the Boer War.

My mom keeps asking what time it is and my dad looks at his watch and tells her, without getting impatient. Everything seems to be going extra slowly.

We pass the road to Carletonville where one of us always says, "That's the way to our old house in Florida. Isn't it?" And then another asks, "When can we go back and see it? Please! Please!"

Right after that turnoff I look to see what's going on at the secret factory where the uranium is kept. You can see it from the road but only mining people know what it is.

We're getting closer. I see Moroka and Orlando in the distance. That's where Grandad worked as a health inspector before he retired. He started out as a blacksmith but he studied and took exams and got a job with the municipality. He took me with him to work once. You have to drive carefully in a native location because the roads are full of potholes and there are only a few street signs. It's smoky and smells bad.

We don't stop at Uncle Charlie's Roadhouse like we normally do, but drive straight through the Southern Suburbs where Mom and Dad grew up. They know all the places and streets there and both went to Forest High. They were both poor but I'm not sure who was the poorest.

Usually we bypass the middle of the city, but today we drive by all the skyscrapers and find parking in a side street across from the General Hospital. We stay put in the car, but Mom rushes right in with her coat and handbag. Afterwards Dad says we can get out and stretch our legs. He tells me to hold Gill's hand.

After ages and ages Mom comes back. She's crying and puts her head on Dad's chest. We were too late, Grandad's dead. He's only been dead half an hour and is still in his bed under a sheet. She lifted it up and saw him dead underneath. Granny would have stopped her, but she was sitting in the waiting room. We stand around crying and patting her while crowds of people walk around us on the pavement.

Gran and Mom are going to "make arrangements" and we are going to Sandown. Ingrid is really crying. She always goes to Gran and Grandad's flat in Townsview for holidays when I go to my other granny. Grandad used to paint pictures on his balcony overlooking the hills.

I sit in the front with Dad. Ingrid and Gill are in the back. We drive down Oxford Road with the palm trees all down the middle and then all the turns through Inanda and at last we come to the gravel road called Catherine Street where my other gran has a smallholding. It's called "Eshowe", which means "wind in the trees" in Zulu.

I open and shut the gate for the car and we go slowly down the winding drive and park under the jacaranda tree. Uncle John opens the front door and I jump out and tell him Grandad has died. My dad looks at me and I know I should have let him tell first.

Ingrid, Gill and I aren't allowed to go to the funeral. Aunty Toff stays to look after us. I walk around the place wishing I'd brought my catapult. I might have got a rock pigeon for Cutwell the gardener to eat. No one shoots them here so it would be easy. They just sit on the slate tiles and look down at you.

The good fruit is finished: only quinces and lemons are left. All the time I'm looking about I keep saying, "Monday the eleventh of May! Monday the eleventh of May!" I'm going to make sure I remember.

The Muscovies quack and flap into the pond when I jump out from behind the bamboo patch. I don't know why Gran keeps them. All they do is quack. She never eats them because she says they're too fatty, and I never see any duck eggs. Anyway, she gets piles of eggs from the chickens and bantams and is always giving them away.

Everything in the summerhouse is packed away for the winter and the swimming pool is drained. I use the steps at the shallow end and walk down the slope to the deepest part. It is like being way down in a big, empty box. I look up and all I see is blue sky and the tops of trees.

I say, "Monday the eleventh of May, 1959!" Down here it echoes and I say it again and again. Next year on this same day I'm going to get my mom alone and say, "Grandad died one year ago, today. I remembered!"

Gill

Often at dinner, after we've eaten, it goes like this: Mom says, "If you keep this up, Kenneth, sowaar you're going to get a slap."

"I didn't do anything. I'm just sitting here!" I'm opposite my mom. Gillian is across the table at her side.

Gill says, "Yes you did! You smile at me and then you pull a silly face," and she begins to cry. I don't even know why I tease her. I can't help it. It seems normal, like the way I tease Ingrid, only more dangerous. Ingrid sits dead still with her hands in her lap. She always sits like that when there's trouble. She makes her face go blank.

My dad pushes his chair back and says, "I've had about enough!" and walks off. He's not fair. Sometimes he teases her with his "little fishes lick the dishes" grace before dinner or says "bwide" instead of "bride" and when she gets angry he says, "Gilly-Bill, I'm just charfing." And that's that, he doesn't get in trouble.

"See what you caused?" Mom says and rings the bell for William to come and clean up the table. She starts grinding Gill's pills between two spoons. Big ones have to be cut in half first, and she's careful that pieces don't fly off, otherwise the dose is wrong.

Gill takes pills for everything, but she won't swallow them. She's afraid of choking, so everything must be ground into powder and mixed with jam, but even then she can make a fuss, especially after dinner when we're all sitting around. She screams that they taste awful and will make her sick and then everyone starts arguing and trying to help.

She has cerebral palsy and is also epileptic and spastic. I'm not sure which came first, or which caused what, but she and her sister got their tubes tangled when they were still inside Mom. They cut off stuff to each other and Gillian's got an empty space in her brain that messed up a lot of things. But not everything.

She weighed only a few pounds when she was born and had to be kept in an incubator at the hospital so she'd grow properly. Her twin was stillborn but we don't know where the hospital buried her. Mom says she could easily have fit in a shoebox.

Gill was pretty, and bundled up she looked normal, but everyone except Mom was scared of carrying her around in case something went wrong.

Right from the beginning she was squint and had one curled-up hand and a twisted foot. No one knows how she's going to turn out, but she keeps trying and she learned to crawl and walk and talk. Mom spends hours teaching her to read. She loves being pushed on the back-yard swing, and has even learned to swing herself. Every time she manages something new we're all happy. It's like a birthday or Christmas.

I think if she walked like us nobody would know the difference, but she has such a limp and she talks so loudly that people look at her and then pretend they didn't.

She drops stuff, gets a fright and starts yelling, "It's not my fault!" Half the time I think she just wants sympathy. When

97

she has tantrums, Ingrid and I are extra careful. It's not funny but it makes me want to laugh. If Mom or Dad see me even smile, they tell me to get outside.

Mom says, "You must be kind and understanding with her. She's frustrated and sick and often unhappy." But it goes on and on all the time, day after day.

Ingrid and I know she has to be spoilt because of being handicapped, but we think it's not fair she gets away with everything. She's only happy when everybody's making a fuss of her.

"Look what they gave me," she says when she comes home from visiting and shows me some brooch. If I don't say something nice, Mom and Dad say it wouldn't kill me to be just a tiny bit kind. And people give her stuff all the time. It's as though they think that if they give presents to a crippled person it proves they are really, really kind. And then they talk loudly to her so everybody can listen. "Oh Gilly, what a pretty Alice band!" or, "Oh Gill, you've got such lovely thick hair!" Stuff like that. In the meantime their kids are sneaking looks at her lace-up boot and calliper. I feel like telling them it's not polite to stare.

It's no one's fault that she's crippled.

She wants me to be a policeman when I grow up so I can look after her properly when we're old. Everyone thinks this is so sweet. It is sweet, sort of, but I never know what I'm supposed to say. Maybe she'll die young. But if she doesn't, who'll look after her when Mom and Dad are dead? I think they want it to be me because I'm the oldest, but Ingrid could do it way better.

Gillian started Strathvaal School a year later than normal kids. She got special permission to go because there are no handicap schools here or in Klerksdorp. She was in Grade One for two years but this year she's very proud because they said she could go to Grade Two.

When we're dropped off by Dad in the morning, either Ingrid or I must walk her to the classroom and make sure she puts her stuff away safely. She tells us not to go fast and talks away. I'm a bit embarrassed if I see my friends watching. As soon as she's in the classroom I push off.

But some days I'm even proud that we've a handicapped person in our family. People look at us as though we know what it's like to be good and sad all the time.

If we go to Potch Dam or the public swimming pool, one of us has to stand around while she plays about where it's shallow. She's slowly learning to swim, and screams and shouts when she floats for just a second with her one water wing.

Strange things always happen to her.

This winter she got a tapeworm. It somehow got in her from bits of raw meat Mom gave us. She has to eat pumpkin seeds to try to kill it and hates that taste as well. I wish we'd kept it private, but somehow Vic Roodt and his dumb sisters know. They say a tapeworm can grow bigger than a mamba and its mouth is open at the back of your throat so it gets your food even before it's in your stomach.

Mom has to check if bits of worm have fallen out in the lavatory. It's disgusting.

Mom believes only one person in the world can help us with Gill, and that's Dr Heymann. He's a specialist for handicapped people and Mom says he's famous even in America. His office is in Johannesburg and Mom takes Gill up there by bus every month. He sees how Gill is doing and then afterwards they sometimes go to the Forest Town School for Spastics so that Gill can have physiotherapy.

I'm used to retarded kids because Mom invites them and their parents to our house. Ing and I have to stand around and be polite. Mrs Worral's boy Johnny can barely sit up. He just sort of leans sideways on the chair as though he's ready to fall over. Mom says, "Poor Johnny is really terribly backward." I never know what he's saying when he talks. Only his mom understands. Anyway, I visited the School for Spastics once and, even though I'm used to it, I'd never seen so many strange-looking kids. My eyes started watering and I knew I was going to burst out laughing but I stuffed my hanky in my mouth and nearly choked.

My dad's friend Dr Visander visits with his deaf and dumb sons. They sit on the couch with dribble running down their chins, making hand signals to each other.

Gill is one of the reasons I've got to go to boarding school. Mom once told me it wasn't fair that we had to grow up around someone who's sick all the time. But I've also heard them say our house is a madhouse. So maybe she and Dad need more peace and quiet.

I stood by the switch until Dad got the focus right and said I could turn off the lights, and then I stretched out on the carpet with Ingrid and Gill. William sat near the kitchen on a chair he'd carried in.

Dad has been busy for ages splicing titles and dates into our short family movies. Now they're all spliced together and tonight we watched the whole long film for the first time – the whole family history from the time he got the Eumig camera until now. White circles run around the screen and the red word "Kodak" appears over and over again.

All of us are standing in the front yard of 143 Van Riebeeck. It is 1956. We have our best clothes on. I look stupid. Ingrid is trying to look pretty.

Gilly was two or three then. She smiles and starts limping slowly toward the camera. I'd forgotten how sick she looked in those days. Besides me, she's the one I notice most in the film. I try to see whether she's getting more normal or not.

There's me fixing a flat tyre on my bike, Ing's doing ballet on the lawn, Mom's talking to the camera and laughing, and Gran and Grandad Smith are visiting us just before he died. Grandad always wore a cardigan.

Mom says they are the last pictures ever taken of him.

Hilary is on film for the first time. She's only two weeks old and everybody has a turn holding her and trying to make her smile. Ingrid pushes her down the driveway and Gill follows behind, pushing her toy pram with one arm. All our holidays on the South Coast are there, all the different cottages. You can see us getting bigger. Gill paddles in the lagoon. Spotty runs along the beach.

The film runs out. The room is lit up by the projector. I look at Gill, sitting with her good arm around her knees, the other one just hanging loose. She's smiling at the screen as though something is still going on.

Sometimes she stops and looks up, but not at anything. She's frozen. She's having a tiny fit, but Mom calls it "a start". Then she begins chattering to herself and forgets what just happened.

She'll never be able to go out on her own. Mom says it's up to us. Our family is all she's got.

Grown-ups

At Christmas and New Year grown-ups have parties every weekend. Sometimes there's more than one party a night, and Mom and Dad go from one to another. There are special dinners too, but cocktail parties are the favourites. The grown-ups drink and dance and sometimes get tipsy or even drunk. We are left at home with a babysitter, but sometimes, if the people have children, they invite Ingrid and me to keep their kids company and we sit in a bedroom somewhere and listen to music, drink Coke and eat crisps. Usually we fall asleep before the end, but once I heard a lady in a nearby room say, "Oh! Okay, but just a kiss."

One family has a cut-glass bowl on the sideboard full to the top with red plastic lions. Thousands of them. You can run your fingers through the bowl. A small lion comes with every bottle of Booth's Gin. On the way home Dad said, "My God! Between the two of them they must polish off a bottle a day."

Mom said, "Steffen! Not in front of the children."

At that same party I heard Elvis Presley singing for the first time. It was a song called "All Shook Up" and I couldn't stop listening. I asked if I could get the record for Christmas, but Dad said no. Elvis was a ducktail. Ducktails didn't respect authority, and they and Teddy boys fought with knuckledusters, bicycle chains and flick knives. He said that there were hoodlums just like that, right here on the mine.

One night some had tried to gatecrash a party of grown-ups, revving their motorbikes outside the house and shouting, but when all the men went outside they had sped away.

But he's not fair. He says Frank Sinatra's a lounge lizard and a bloody crooner even though Mom likes him. And he makes squarking noises and walks outside when she listens to Nat King Cole. His favourites are Mario Lanza and Mantovani.

The phone rang just after lunch and Mom answered. It was one of those quiet phone calls where the other person talks and talks. Then she said, "I'll be ready."

She started rushing about, putting on Sunday clothes and make-up, brushing her hair and telling me to stop asking questions. She told William to watch us and that she'd be back in a tick.

Gordon de Villiers and Ken Hinks pulled up at the gate and got out of their car. She walked down the gravel drive on her high heels and they all drove off. Both men were my dad's bosses and I didn't like them. I did my best not to play with their kids.

She got home at the same time as my dad and they stood talking before he put his arm around her shoulders and they walked up to the house. She looked fine to me.

We asked what happened and she said she had to tell some poor woman on Kervel Road that her husband was dead. He'd fallen asleep or had a heart attack or something while driving back from Welkom and crashed. Just like that. Alive one minute, dead the next. The wife sat there and said to my mom, "What am I supposed to do now?"

I asked why she was the one who had to go and she said the mine always took a woman with them to comfort the wife if a man was hurt or killed. Usually it was Mrs De Villiers, but she was away, so Gordon called her.

"They thought I could do it. I take it as a compliment," she said.

If you're not married you live in the Single Quarters and park on the street, but everyone else has a house and a garage, and if you get promoted you get a bigger house on a better street. Every time Dad's promoted Mom says, "Your father is a brilliant man. He's much cleverer than his bosses."

She's always saying things like that. She even thinks he looks like Gregory Peck; I don't know why.

Up on the hill the managers and assistant managers and mine secretaries and chief engineers have their huge houses with swimming pools and fancy gardens. Some have orchards and grapevines, looked after by gangs of natives sent by the mine. The managers even have gate guards all day and all night.

Their kids think they're special, and if I'm forced to go up there to play, I wander off by myself and pull carrots from the vegetable garden and wash them in the pool when no one's looking. Then I stuff whole bunches of grapes in my mouth.

You can tell from where a kid lives whether your dad is his dad's boss or his dad is your dad's boss. We yell at each other, "My dad's going to fire your dad!" Then the other kid yells back, "No, he can't; he needs a reason. And anyway I don't care, I'm still gonna donner you."

Almost all my friends are from around here, so they are all Harties kids. My dad is their dad's boss if they don't work underground. If they do, someone else is their dad's boss. I hardly ever say it, that my dad's their dad's boss, but I know it.

My dad says kids shouldn't worry about who their dad's boss is.

I got interested in chess and taught myself to play from a library book. Dad knew a bit, but after a few games he got bored and told me he knew someone from the assay office who was supposed to be a chess wizard. Dad said he'd check and see if the man would teach me.

One night, after dinner we walked down the road to the man's house. Dad told me that before the war this man had been a teacher in one of those countries that now belonged to Russia. Most of his family were killed in concentration camps but he'd escaped to Denmark and somehow got here. I was not to ask him questions about the war.

Dad introduced me at the front door and left. The lounge was so dark I could barely see the chessboard set out on the coffee table. Orchestra music was playing on the radiogram.

The man hardly spoke, but when he did he sounded like a foreigner in a film. He beat me so quickly that, for a second, I thought he'd cheated. He showed me how to castle and then explained why it was sometimes a good move. You could tell he was once a teacher. He explained exactly.

A lady came in with a plate of biscuits. She wore a long dress and slippers. I stood up and she nodded and smiled but didn't say anything. Not to either of us. Maybe she couldn't speak English. Then she went out. She was his wife, I suppose. But she could have been someone else.

After he beat me some more, he said we'd played enough for one day and I should go home and practise. He lent me a book and showed me how you write down the moves to prove you'd solved the problem and then he walked me back to our gate in the dark. He wore a black hat that made him seem like a person from long ago.

I went back a few times, but then I stopped going. It was too quiet there and I was useless. Each time it was easier to beat me. He kept his hands on his knees except when he made a move and he never lifted his head, even when he said "Check".

I had warts everywhere. They were all over my hands, my elbows, my neck and even one in my nose. This was the worst one, and it kept getting bigger and bigger and I could see people looking at it. Kids said I should stop kissing frogs.

Mom tried putting some black stuff on them but all it did was burn, so she forced me to go to the doctor. He had his office right above the butcher at the shopping centre. She held me while he injected me between my lip and nose with a huge needle. I screamed but he just told me to be quiet.

Then he started burning the wart with something that looked like what a welder uses. It was smoking right under my nose and smelled awful. When I screamed again he grabbed my head from behind like he was going to crush it. He left a black hole where the wart had been and it took ages to look normal. On the way home I told Mom that he was useless and I'd never go back, but she said I'd do as I was told.

Randall and Allister's dad got rid of the rest of my warts. Mr Compton worked underground and always had a pipe in his mouth. He dried his tobacco in saucers on the window-sill in his back yard because it was too wet straight from the can. He saw my warts and said he could make them disappear. I told Mom and Dad, and Dad said he thought all the witch doctors on the mine were black. They both laughed.

I went one Saturday anyway. Mr Compton shooed the boys from the house and told me to sit on the old couch. Then he made me promise not to tell anyone the magic words, because if I did, the warts might come back, but even worse. What he did, he'd learned from his grandfather in Cornwall when he was a boy.

He said the special words in a singsong way. They sounded foreign. He rubbed some yellow stuff that he kept in a little bottle on all the warts and said to leave it there until I had my bath.

My warts slowly shrunk and shrunk and then went away for good.

Dad says it's ballyhooey and a coincidence and not scientific and Mom says it's the medicine the real doctor gave me. I don't care what they say; I believe it was him.

Walter van Rooyen worked in the reduction works and was a friend of my dad. I called him Uncle Walter. He taught me to fire real guns way before I got the Gecado pellet gun for Christmas. We'd drive out to the slimes dam on a Sunday afternoon and he'd try to shoot meerkats and hawks, resting his rifle on the open window. He had to be careful because natives were always walking across the veld on their way to one of the shafts or on their way back to the compounds.

I could tell my dad didn't like it, but he didn't stop me going. Uncle Walter had all kinds of rifles and pistols and shot at competitions, called Bisleys, where he got mad if he didn't get a bull's-eye every time. His wife was a friend of my mom. She was always smoking and putting on lipstick. Ingrid loved her and used to walk up to their house with me on Saturday afternoons and learn about make-up and stuff.

Uncle Walter turned their garage into a workshop. Once he built a little revolver hardly bigger than a matchbox that fired real bullets. I watched for weeks as he put it together. He had drawings and turned tiny parts on his lathe. He let me be there when he tested it. He clamped it in a vice and put some string around the trigger. We stood outside the door and he pulled the thread. It fired the tiny bullet perfectly.

My mom was always saying his wife, Anita, was unhappy, and then one day she completely disappeared. She even left her kid behind. Mom said she was hiding at her parents' in Barkly West. There was big trouble. Mom was whispering on the phone. One day, after work, Uncle Walter met Dad for drinks at the Three Fountains Hotel and told him right in the bar that if my mom didn't stay out of his business he would shoot Dad or Mom, I'm not sure which. I think Dad said he had a revolver in his pocket.

He was transferred the next day and we never saw him or his kid again.

I asked my mom why Anita van Rooyen left her kid behind and my mom said, "Some women are just not cut out for motherhood. She made a terribly hard choice. She'll live with it the rest of her life."

People are always in our house asking my mom for advice and help. They think she knows everything and she feels sorry for nearly everyone. I wish she'd tell them to buzz off and just look after us.

Up North

Dad comes in from work. He has his jacket over his arm and is loosening his tie. Before he even says hello he says, "Phew, what's that smell? Fish? Onions?" And he pulls a face.

He hates any cooking that smells strange. When he was in the Middle East during the war, he nearly starved because food smelled different and didn't taste like anything he was used to. He ended up with pellagra, which left white patches on his shins along with the dents from hockey sticks. He was even in hospital for a while.

Mom sometimes says, "Oh come on, Steffen! Tell them about coming in to land at Gibraltar! Or about Oeschger flying the plane to the tune of 'Lili Marlene', or about the waterspout, or about Geoff depth-charging a British sub!" And sometimes he does.

Mostly his stories are funny or about big mess-ups. He never brags. He was training to be a pilot but he landed his Tiger Moth ten feet above the "deck" so they sent him to navigator school instead.

When my dad talks about the aerodrome at St Jean's in Palestine, I always imagine my mom being there, because Jean is her name. I imagine the Crusader fort, and her waiting for him, like in a film, even though they only met after the war was over. She was a typist and he was on the mines.

Tons of men working here were "up north" during the war. Jack van Eyssen's hair went white in one night when the

Russians were going to shoot him and his crew because they thought they were Nazis. Stewart Finney, Hilary's godfather, was a Spitfire pilot and fought over the Western Desert. He's still got a piece of bullet in his hip. And another friend of my dad has a limp because when he was in uniform, traitors from the Ossewabrandwag, who supported the Germans, threw him off a bridge near Park Station. Tons of people on the mine were in the Army Engineers. They built roads and bridges and bulldozed landing strips all over the place.

My dad was a navigator, and when a kid asks me what that is, I explain, but say he was a bomb aimer as well, just so they know he was really fighting.

At school we ask each other, "What did your dad do in the war?" If someone says they don't know, you know their dad didn't do anything.

I build models of Second World War planes from kits. I start by gluing together the two halves of the fuselage and finish by making sure the ailerons can flap and then clicking the transparent cockpit cover over the pilot. I've learned to use a toothpick to put on the glue, otherwise it messes up the plastic and sticks to your fingers. I paint the top of the plane in green and khaki swirls and the underside in pale blue, and then I soak the decals in a saucer of water and slip them off the paper and onto the right spots.

I have planes all over my room, some mounted on clear plastic stands and some just sitting on their landing gear on the windowsill, ready to take off. I've built Stukas and Hurricanes, 109s and Wellingtons. Even biplanes from the First World War. I've got at least twenty but nobody makes model kits of Dad's plane, the Ventura – not Airfix, Revell, Frog or any of the others.

Crews called the Ventura "The Pig" because it was slow and hopeless in a fight and could be shot down in a second. But Dad says it was a good bomber and anti-sub plane and anyway they didn't have a choice.

I ask him about fighters, about Messerschmitts especially, but he saw one only once, far off, and straightaway they dived into cloud for cover, and thank God too, he says, because if they'd been seen it would have been "tickets" and he wouldn't have been standing in front of me.

He lets me look at his logbook if I sit with it flat on the table. And also his big photo album with hundreds of pictures of the war. He's written all the place names in white ink on the black paper, and as he turns the pages he says the name of someone he's forgotten and shakes his head. He talks about Yanks and Gyppos and Eyeties. It looks like nearly everyone in the Air Force had a moustache.

He's told me heaps about the war, about Tobruk and Churchill, D-Day, Monte Cassino and Stalingrad, but when I think about war, I mainly think about aeroplanes because that's what he was in. He volunteered to fly and if there's another war that's what I'd try for.

After a whole year's training he flew up Africa in a DC-3, all the way from Pretoria to Cairo. It took ten days and there they changed to a Ventura and made the last hop to St Jean's.

The main work of his squadron was protecting convoys from submarines and bombing harbours all over "the Med". In one year he moved from Palestine to Egypt to Cyprus, then

Oran, Cyrenaica, Gibraltar, Sardinia and Tarquinia in Italy. Pasted in his logbook is a special page where his squadron commander says he was "an excellent, outstanding, all-round navigator".

On the eleventh of January 1944 the logbook says he flew night escort for a convoy, code-named "Rose", which was sailing from Famagusta to Haifa. His plane had a crew of four: pilot, navigator, wireless operator and gunner. Everything went smoothly. The next night they took off again to cover the same convoy.

This time the logbook is different. It says *Lightning, Blips, Waterspout, Dead Starboard Engine, Single Engine Landing*. It's written in red ink, like all the night flying.

He told me how the pilot had battled to keep in formation above the ships. The weather was terrible and the radar was behaving strangely. Breaking out of clouds, they saw a water-spout dead ahead, thousands of feet high and still towering above them. He said it was black and white in the moonlight and very beautiful.

They banked sharply. The plane was buffeted back and forth and a lightning strike made all the instruments useless. Then an engine gave out. The pilot steadied the plane and tried to gain altitude. They prepared for the worst, jettisoning the depth charges, checking their parachutes and readying the dinghies. My dad said he was terribly afraid but plotting a course using astro navigation kept him busy. He said it was worst for Kruger, the gunner, who had nothing to do. They flew on in darkness, just over the water, on one engine.

The plane came in low from the sea. St Jean d'Acre and the

bay were still dark but they could make out the outline of the Pasha Mosque. Fraser, the wireless op, tried to talk directly to the tower as Oeschger made a slow, wide turn, all the while descending, and then settled into his approach.

My dad stared at the feathered propellor. They were over the fields now and barely noticed the fire truck at the end of the runway. Oeschger brought her down; she bounced a few times, skidded a little and stopped. A cheer went up inside and Oeschger grinned and stuck up a thumb. Everyone smiled at everyone else.

They climbed out the door, stepped down off the wing and stood side by side. The sun was coming up. Dad's toes were curled and stiff in his flying boots. He stamped his feet, stretched and took out his smokes.

Natives

William Kamanga is the native I know best. Long ago, before I'd even started school, he came to our back door and asked for work. He stood on the step with his head down and his hands together while my mother looked at his papers and asked him questions he could hardly understand. But she decided to give him a try and he went off to fetch his suitcase from somewhere. She said he had a nice smile and that Nyasa boys were clean and worked hard.

She showed him the servant's room behind the garage, gave him sheets, a blanket, a mug and some plates, and started training him. She taught him how to dust, how to wash the dishes, how to polish the silver and all the other things. He's small and my mom's old apron hangs over his knees. On Sundays, his day off, he wears his best clothes, sits on a chair outside his room and has visitors. We have to remember not to ask him to do anything.

He's shown me how to plait grass and thin branches to make wips and snares to catch all kinds of animals and birds. He also gives me the Rhodesia and Nyasaland stamps from his letters. They're all the same size and have a picture of the Queen, but in different colours for different amounts.

Now and then he asks Mom to post a small box of fish hooks to his family, who live on the shore of Lake Nyasa. It's so full of fish that hooks are more valuable than money.

Mary, his wife, knocked on the back door one day. She'd

come all the way from Nyasaland and somehow sneaked across the Limpopo River, even though it's full of crocodiles. It took her weeks to get here, and then after only a few days the police caught her on the road without a pass and sent her back home. As soon as she got there, she turned around and did it all again. She stayed for months and spent the whole time in the back yard because she was afraid to go out.

When Mom and Dad aren't home, I'll take my pellet gun or cattie and try to kill a rock pigeon or dove for William. If I get one and it tumbles down into the gutter, I climb on the roof and wrap it in newspaper so blood doesn't drip everywhere. I'd get in big trouble if they caught me. They'd probably take away my gun for good.

William especially likes Mom and Ingrid, but he's nervous of Dad and always has tea and *The Star* ready when he comes back from the reduction works. Mom says that natives naturally look up to their chief.

At school, South African history is one part of Cultural Studies and most of it is about how whites and natives have fought one another from the beginning.

Jan van Riebeeck came to the Cape in 1652 and found Hottentots walking up and down the beach looking for mussels and perlemoen and squabbling with each other. There were also Bushmen hiding up in the mountains, but that was all.

The Dutch had to bring slaves from Malaya because the Hottentots wouldn't work and stole everything. Later the Trekboers started going deeper into the country to escape from the English missionaries who wanted to end slavery and the English governors who kept bossing them around. There they ran into the Xhosa, who stole their cattle. So the Boers started the Great Trek and had to fight for their lives all the way to the Limpopo River. The tribes, especially the Zulus, tried to turn them back. But they couldn't. Luckily the Transvaal and Orange Free State were nearly empty and they formed their own countries.

Now Europeans are trying to get along with the natives. The government is going to give each tribe their own country. And they will also allow natives to come and work on the mines and in our houses so they can send money back to their families. Their countries will be called "Bantustans".

But some natives want more. They want to share everything, one for one. The government says that they can have all they want, but back in their own Homelands, not here. The natives say all South Africa belongs to them, even more than to us. "Over our dead bodies!" say the whites, especially the Afrikaners.

My mom thinks that if you call a native a "kaffir" or a "munt", you prove you're just common. She's strict about how we behave with them. "They have feelings just like you. Use your manners!" She says, "Say 'please' and 'thank you'. Don't push in front of them in a queue, even if a white man tells you to come right to the front."

She often says that Robert Sobukwe is handsome. I look at who is listening. I didn't know you could even say that about natives.

Grandad is just like her. He works in Sophiatown and Moroka but he won't carry a gun even though the municipality says he must. He thinks the people there are dignified and work hard.

But my dad has different ideas. He believes natives have a separate mentality. He says it will take a hundred years to bring them to our level. And he thinks it was a mistake to allow them to drive, especially trucks. "They have no respect for life. They're fatalists."

Every white person has something to tell you about natives. Gran says they have too many children. "They want to be looked after when they're old." And she's sure the younger ones are becoming cheekier.

One of my aunts believes that if they aren't watched, they stop working. "Just look at the garden boys at the fence, smoking and chatting away. Time and money mean absolutely nothing to them."

The Compton brothers, or maybe it was Dessington, told me that some native burglars take off their clothes and smear themselves with margarine before they break in. Then they're too slippery to grab and can easily jump through the window and run down the road.

People are always saying, "Look what happened in Kenya with the Mau Mau!" or, "Look what happened in Katanga! If they ran things here it would be a complete bloodbath!"

An uncle says that natives either want to drive us all into the sea or hack us to death with pangas. He once said at Christmas lunch, right in front of everyone, "A kaffir is a kaffir and will always be a kaffir."

My dad says his brother is ignorant and we should ignore him.

I notice how natives look at us. I think that even the ones that are nice don't really like us a lot. But some don't pretend anything. They look straight at you without a smile. When a white man tells them what to do, they make a clicking sound, turn away and say something in their own language.

We speak extra slowly to natives to make sure they understand what we want, but there are Europeans who shout and push them around. Mr Saville once punched the garden boy in the face because he came to work drunk.

My dad has a friend, Mr Curtis, who also flew in bombers up north. The head office in Joburg transferred him down to Virginia in the Free State because they thought he was a "hothead" and too mixed up in politics.

He visited us in the school holidays with his wife and three kids. After they left my dad said that his friend was going to run in the election for the Progressive Party. Dad said people could say what they liked about him, but he had guts and principles. Mr Curtis believes natives should be like us, have the vote and everything. Even live right next door. There are a few whites like that, but people call them "commies" or "kaffir boeties".

My parents went overseas to Greece and Italy and England at the beginning of the year. My mom had never been before and she wrote aerogrammes almost every single day, telling us which temple or church or museum they were seeing and what strange food they ate.

Then suddenly Sharpeville happened.

The police said they were attacked but some newspapers

say that most of the dead and wounded were shot in the back while running away.

Here in Stillies the police drove through the streets in their Black Marias with natives singing and shouting in the cages on the back. Some were bleeding. They'd refused to carry their passes and were going to jail.

Gran was taking care of us and we sat around listening to the news on the radio. People phoned to see if we were safe because they knew we were alone. She made us draw the curtains even before it got dark, and locked the doors. I had the pellet gun and hockey stick under my bed in case I had to fight, and lay in bed listening to the sounds outside my window. I was scared but I wasn't the only one.

In her letters Mom said it sounded pretty grim.

She flew home first, because Dad had to go on to Canada for a mining conference. After he got back he said some Americans had offered him a good job on a mine in Colorado, and for a time they spoke about emigrating. I didn't say much, but I would have liked to give it a try.

Strathvaal

This Friday will be the last day of school and the beginning of the holidays. I wish I was coming back to Strathvaal next year for Standard Five but I'm going to boarding school in Kimberley.

Last night we had the school play and prize-giving. On the cover of the programme was the school badge and our motto, "Golden Future". Inside were the names of the kids who had won prizes and other stuff.

We've been rehearsing *The Magic Carpet* with Mrs Crosby forever. There are ten acts; each is about a different country. I'm in the one about Russia and we sing "The Volga Boatmen's Song" and pretend to row the boat while looking at the audience.

Estelle van Zyl is the flamenco dancer. She's in Standard Five. Her hair is pitch-black like Prince Valiant's and I stare at her and wish she'd stare at me but she never does, even when I stand in her way. I don't know what to do. Her eyes are brown with lots of white. She clicks her castanets over her head and smiles at Larry Wittstock. He combs his hair with Brylcreem and acts like he's a grown-up or something.

Last night she had proper make-up round her eyes and lipstick and a Spanish dress and everything. I could hardly breathe. I felt like I did at Ingrid's birthday, when her friend Sandra asked me to give her a lift on my bike. She sat on the crossbar as we went down the road and she suddenly turned and kissed me and giggled. Her hair was tickling my face and she wriggled between my arms. I hardly knew I was riding a bike.

Before the play, we sang the National Anthem and then Mr Jones read from the Bible and the choir sang the Lord's Prayer. Afterwards some person from Potch gave a speech about how the youth of today is being led astray somehow. All us kids were sitting at the front of the hall on the floor. It was so uncomfortable. The grown-ups had chairs. Near the end the prizes were given out. I got one for being first in class in 4A. Aileen Dinsdale got the same thing for 4B.

The choir sang "Bless this School" and we all went home. In the car Mom said, "Kenneth, you should keep the programme. For the future. It's your last year here and you got First Prize too. It'll be something to look back on."

I remember the first morning we moved from the old school to Strathvaal. All the English-speaking kids lined up on the playground. Our teachers were fussing, telling us not to forget anything and to be quiet. Some Afrikaner shouted, "Voetsek, rooinek!" and one of the big English kids yelled back, "Totsiens, rockspider!" We all laughed.

They walked us in two long rows, past the Three Fountains Hotel and the town's swimming pool and up the hill. The teachers stopped the traffic every time we had to cross a road. Dogs barked and people waved.

We were glad to leave Stilfontein Laerskool and all the Dutchies behind. It was so crowded there that some kids even had to go to school in the afternoon, and English and

Afrikaans gangs were always arguing and fighting in the playground. I used to hang about the cloakroom or near the classroom during breaks waiting for the bell to ring, and at the end of school I ran home with Neville Smook. We both lived really close, at the bottom of Van Riebeeck.

But Strathvaal was a brand-new school. We walked into classrooms that had never been used before. The blackboards were shiny and the inkwells were pure white. The fences weren't even finished and the playing field was still just a piece of veld.

I started on the ground floor in Standard One. I was seven. My teacher was called Mrs Kirk. Since I've been here I've only been in big trouble once. Last year in the first term of Standard Three I was called down to the principal's office. I sat with the school secretary for ages trying to think what I'd done wrong, and then Mr Jones opened his door and told me to come in. He made me stand in front of him while he sat at his desk. He just stared at me. Mom and Dad call him "Rolly", but he's mean and thinks people from Wales are better than anybody else. He looked at me and said he'd heard I was clever but very lazy and I'd better start working or "there will be consequences". I nearly cried going out and had to wait a bit on the stairs before I went back into class.

At home I didn't say anything, but when Mom said I seemed to be very quiet, I knew she was the one who'd got Jones to yell at me. She's always telling me to do my home-work, but when I say I'm already finished, she says I'm a fibber, and Dad said my last report was just average. When he says that, he means useless.

But school is so boring. The teachers tell you the same thing over and over again until you nearly fall asleep. Some take a swipe at you with a ruler if you do something they don't like.

So I was forced to learn to do homework and anyway it was easy. At the end of last year they gave me a Progress Prize.

I've biked to school a few times, racing across the whole town in the early morning without stopping, but I get here way too soon and end up eating my lunch sandwich and feeling hungry all day. Mostly, though, Dad drops us all off on his way to work. Ingrid's in Standard Two now and has Mrs Louw. She's the scariest teacher in the school. Gill is still in the Grades because Mom says she needs to catch up, but we all know she can't really do schoolwork. Dad fetches us again on his way home for lunch. Then he lies on the bed and has forty winks before going back to the reduction works.

The Standard Threes', Fours' and Fives' classrooms are upstairs and that's where I'm now.

I sit near the back of 4A. Mr Chater, our teacher, hardly ever speaks to me, but after I got full marks for an arithmetic test he asked how much time I spent on my homework. And another time he asked me what I was reading when I burst out laughing by mistake. I told him *William and the Moon Rocket* and the whole class laughed.

From the windows you can see the Margaret headgear and the Stillies' rock pile. If you stretch your neck, you can also see the smoke over Khumba location. That's where all the natives live and I wouldn't go there by myself at night for a million pounds.

I have fun in class. Some of us use small peashooters all the time. We fire at each other, but not at the girls because they tell the teacher and he stops everything until someone owns up. Sometimes I even use a fly cattie and fire wet paper wads across the room and onto the blackboard, but only if Chater's not here.

I invented this special trick: I take a bit of Scotch tape and wet the sticky side with spit and roll the glue off in one long piece. It's yellowish and looks like a piece of snot. Next I put it in my nose and leave a small piece dangling out. I poke the kid sitting in front of me and when he looks around I point to my nose and slowly pull it out, show it to him and then put it in my mouth and say "yum, yum" very quietly.

Afterwards I quickly show the kid how the trick works. Otherwise he'll tell everyone I ate snot and I won't be able to prove I didn't.

Afrikaans is my worst subject. I hate it. Right through the Easter holidays my aunt forced me to read a book called *Lena se Skulpies* every single day. All I can remember is something about fig jam on slices of brown bread. But I'm all right in the other subjects: Arithmetic, English, Cultural Studies, Scripture, Arts and Crafts and Handwriting.

We have one "small break" and one "big break". Some days we choose gangs that chase each other but mainly we play games. Marbles is my favourite. I always carry a small bag of glassies and a couple of ghoens and I'll play "fish" or "keepie four" or even "keepie ten" if someone asks me. I'm good at it, nearly one of the best at the school. You always have to ask, "Whose game is it?" Then they decide if they'll let you in. Lots of kids won't let me in because I win a lot. They say, "No, not de Kok! Not him."

For no reason everyone suddenly stops playing marbles and starts with tops or yo-yos. But we play stick cricket all the time, usually "one hand one bounce" and "leggy", or we tease girls till they run to the teacher to tell. Then we hide. If it's raining hard we just stand outside the classroom in the corridor and make a racket.

Some days in winter the wind blows so hard that the dust stings your legs and everyone walks backwards so they don't get sand in their eyes. Teachers huddle together and whisper, as though everything is secret.

Today we carried the mat from the shed, rolled it out on the bare pitch and nailed it down. We hammered in the wickets and got everything ready. Jones picked two teams that he said were evenly matched. The other team couldn't get De Waal or Dudley Thomson out so I didn't get a chance to bat, but I bowled two overs and got Allister to hit an easy catch to mid-on.

My dad came to watch because it was my last game and afterwards he said, "Well, my boy, that's that!" Jones walked over and shook my hand and said, "Good luck at the new school. You'll do well!"

I bent down to pull up my socks so they couldn't see my eyes.

Kimberley

Leaving Stillies by myself is the biggest thing that's happened to me. They decided I needed to go to boarding school, and because those schools start Maths and Latin and other stuff before high school, I had to go for Standard Five. I'm not even going to finish primary school here.

At the beginning of the year my dad drove me to Johannesburg to see St Stithians, a Methodist boarding school in Bryanston. It was on the edge of the countryside and had a proper grass cricket pitch. Between the dormitories and classrooms were big trees and hedges and lawn. We looked all over the place and my dad spoke to the headmaster in his office. Uncle John lives close by the school and I could have gone to him on weekends.

Dad didn't say much on the way back but then he told Mom he'd decided against it because it was too liberal. He said he thought a school should have discipline, but I know he thinks I'm a ninny and need toughening up.

Then they asked if I'd go to Christian Brothers College in Kimberley. They'd never seen it, but Mom knew someone who'd sent their kid. She said he liked it. I said I supposed so. There was no other choice except for Potch High and it, some people said, wasn't any good.

Gran and Uncle John are going to pay half the fees. It's not an expensive school, but it's also not cheap.

I've seen photos of the Big Hole in the *Cassell's Encyclopaedia*.

Ropes dangled over the edge and hundreds of people were climbing down the sides and standing at the bottom. Dad told me it was on the edge of the Kalahari Desert and as hot as hell. His mom had grown up there and even eaten horsemeat during the Siege of Kimberley.

They decided that I'd go by train the first time, but from Johannesburg not from Klerksdorp. I'd never been on a train. You sleep on bunk beds and when you wake up you're there.

In November Mom started sewing nametags in all my new clothes so that my stuff wouldn't be mixed up or lost. She'd always cut my nails with clippers after my bath but now she made me do it. Dad taught me to knot my tie and I practised in front of the mirror. The tie was green and blue and gold and it came out skew most of the time but they said it would do, and my blazer was way too big but Mom said I'd soon grow into it. Just about all my stuff was brand-new. William showed me how to polish my shoes and how to put whiting on my takkies.

Dad painted my name on a steel trunk and bought me a combination lock for my locker. I practised opening it and wrote the numbers on a tiny piece of paper.

The closer it got to Christmas, the more scared I got. I was worried that when I got there I'd ask to come home, but Mom said I'd be fine. She said they wouldn't allow bullying.

"You'll be surprised how quickly you'll adapt," she said.

I worried I might start screaming at the station and have to be carried onto the train. She said I'd have to be brave. But bravery is like standing on the roof and not looking down, just jumping off. I can't do it.

It won't be the same here when I come back. My friends will all be at Klerksdorp High and they'll get new friends. And the Cape schools don't even have the same holidays as here, and from next year even Ingrid will be gone to boarding school in Johannesburg. We'll all be together only at Christmas. Hilary has just started walking and talking and being interesting.

I'm going to miss everything. Even my yard will hardly be my yard any more.

On my last night Mom came and lay with me for a bit. She snuggled close and kissed me and said she was going to miss me a lot and that I'd better go to sleep because the next day was going to seem very long.

Dad got a porter to take the trunk. We went to the luggage place where we showed my ticket and paid and got a piece of paper. Dad said I'd better not lose it. We went downstairs, way down to the trains. It was already night down there, the lights were on and trains were steaming in and out. People were pushing and rushing everywhere. We found the proper platform and saw boys in the same uniform standing around with parents. Most were way bigger than me. Some had straw hats and were as big as men, with moustaches and everything. They stared at me and then stared at someone else.

My mom and dad spoke to a Brother for a while. She said he seemed nice. I looked down at my shoes. Ingrid stood next to me. She knew what was going to happen, I could tell.

Conductors started blowing whistles. Somebody, then everybody, said the train was going to leave. I felt sick. Boys started climbing on. I was blubbing. Mom held me tight and kissed me on the top of the head. She was also crying but smiling too. I kissed Ingrid and Dad. I could hardly see them and I was losing my breath. "Stop now, Kenneth! Off you go, darling." Mom gave me a little push.

Two boys were in the compartment. They'd pulled down the window and were leaning out, talking to their families. I wiped my face with both my sleeves. I could just see Ingrid over their shoulders. She waved as the train started moving and then I saw Mom for a split second before she was gone.

During the night I kept waking up as the train rattled along. There was a taste of soot in my mouth. It started getting light and as I peeped out we crossed over a bridge and a river. One kid said, "It's just Warrenton. We've still got half an hour. Close the effin blind."

We came slowly into Kimberley as the sun was coming up. The station had a red corrugated roof and pillars. It looked like a place in a cowboy film. On one side was veld and on the other, right up against the road, small houses with long verandas and no front yards. The train squeaked and hissed and stopped. Boys pushed into the corridor, knotting their ties and tying their laces, and jumped down. I stood on the platform waiting to see what I had to do next.

Fathers and Sons (2012)

My eldest son, Steffen, is named after my father. He has worked for Médecins sans Frontières for years. Once, when he was on his way to Goma in the Congo, I plaited a chain of wild grapevine and he climbed into the old wolf maple on the driveway and hung it there for me as a talisman for his safe return.

Now he's working for the International Commission of the Red Cross in Israel, visiting and advocating for detainees and long-term prisoners.

I flew from Montreal to visit him just before Christmas.

Yesterday morning we drove from Tel Aviv to Jerusalem, parked and walked into the old city through the Damascus Gate. Directly we were in a maze of narrow passages, jostled by Arabs pushing loaded barrows between the market stalls, and hemmed in by throngs of pilgrims walking and singing hymns in myriad languages. Narrow balconies on both sides almost blocked out the sky. We passed through a security checkpoint and looked down on the Mount of Olives and the immense bone-pale graveyard stretching to the heavens.

In the shadow of the great wall, a path wandered between small neglected cemeteries; time had sanded away much of the writing on the mausoleums and tombstones. Feral cats watched us from piles of fallen masonry. Stef asked a Palestinian man for directions and they began an animated conversation. When I asked what they had talked about, he laughed and said, "He wanted to know how come I spoke Arabic with a Moroccan accent."

We came through the metal detectors at the Dung Gate and stood by the Wailing Wall, but when we tried to climb the stairs to see the Al-Aqsa Mosque and the Dome of the Rock, soldiers turned us back. It was Friday and off limits for non-Muslims.

From here the skyline of the old city could be seen and I pointed to the stone- and clay-domed rooftops, the spires, bell towers and minarets: "Grandad was here in the war and took photographs of all of this from the air. It looks the same, even though it was so long ago."

"Yes," he said, "Gran showed me his war albums when I visited last year."

"He was flying from an aerodrome called St Jean's. I wonder where it was? If there's anything left?"

I felt the implacable flow of time. Seventy years have been swept over the falls and into the void since he flew over this city. What does my son, standing beside me, know about my father? And then the lonely thought: what will his children, in turn, know about me?

Today we are driving to Akko, before we cross into Palestine where Stef will visit colleagues. The security wall sealing off the West Bank slips by and he points out Kishon prison, close to the highway but hidden by trees. I ask him again how the work is going and he describes his weekday workload and says the mental health of the long-term prisoners is a major concern. He isn't specific; confidentiality might be the most important reason that the Red Cross is the only foreign organisation allowed access to prisoners here.

We are just outside Akko when he pulls out a scrap of paper and reads as he drives. "I can't believe I've kept this a secret," he says.

I ask him what he means.

"Never mind, I've got to concentrate. I got these directions off the internet and it's kinda complicated," he says. "I'm taking you somewhere before we go into town. I can't believe you can't guess!"

He smiles, but I'm nonplussed. Still jet-lagged, I wonder what we are doing.

We turn off the highway onto a minor road and then almost immediately he slows and steers down a slight incline to a track that skirts a fallow, waterlogged field. There are trees on the far side and low hills behind that. We follow the tracks of a single vehicle through potholes and puddles and past a derelict guard tower.

He slows, stops and switches off the engine. "You see those trees?" He points: "There! Right behind them; that's the old aerodrome. Grandad's!"

I hear him but can't understand. "The St Jean's aerodrome!" he says.

I stare unseeing for a moment, then shivers pass up and down my arms and I hear myself sob. He puts his hand on my back and after a while he says, "I can't believe you didn't figure it out."

I say, "Thanks so much for this, my boy."

We get out of the car and stand by the runway. It's broken up in parts but still wide, straight and so long that the farthest end disappears in the winter haze.

When my father was coaxed into talking about flying, he softened, became almost cheerful. His memories brought out a youthfulness that we hardly ever saw. Mom always said that the war years were the happiest of his life.

I walk out onto the hard, flat surface and look about. On one side is the ruin of a building; weeds and saplings have pushed through the concrete floor. I think it might have been the control tower, and the staggered rows of trees behind it a windbreak.

And then I recognise the trees. Bluegums! The ragged eucalyptus trees of my boyhood.

The past is as vivid as the here and now. I'm watching a home movie; the clouds are bright, the sky is dark, and out over the sea the Ventura is just a speck. I hear the drone of the engine and I watch as the plane makes a wide, slow turn, levels out and comes in to land. The film jumps off the sprockets and flaps around; the reel spins and stops. Empty nothing fills the screen. Dad says, "Can someone get the light?"

Acknowledgements

Thanks to Peter Carey, Daniel de Kok and Stan Dragland who read the manuscript, made suggestions and offered encouragement.

I am greatly indebted to Ivan Vladislavić for his insight into an early version of the manuscript and for providing me with a path forward.

The thoughtfulness, vigilance, and kindness of Tony Morphet and Karen Press were of inestimable value.

To Alfred LeMaitre, who edited the manuscript, and Caren van Houwelingen, my publisher: deep gratitude.

Way, way more than thanks to Carolyn Smart.

My sister Ingrid de Kok, more than sixty years on, still offers her hand, walks me down the passage and switches on the light.

Born in 1949, Kenneth de Kok spent his boyhood in Stilfontein, a mining town now in North West Province. After boarding school in Kimberley, conscription, and three years studying at the University of the Witwatersrand, he left South Africa in 1971 to avoid further military service. He lived and worked in the UK and Holland without documentation before immigrating to Canada in 1978. Self-employed in the kitchen cabinet business, he lives in the countryside of Eastern Ontario. He is married to the Canadian poet Carolyn Smart, and has three sons. He regularly visits South Africa where his mother and three sisters live.